Endorsements

No Tears for Dad is a down-to-earth, poignantly written tale of one man's abusive childhood and its impact on him as a father and son. Chock-full of hard-won wisdom, this must-read invites us to forgive those who've deeply hurt us—including ourselves. The reader can't help but lean in to hear the cry of Cruz's heart as he openly shares his pain, mistakes, and personal story of redemption. His journey from brokenness to healing is breathtakingly beautiful and transparently raw.

Dr. Katherine Hutchinson-Hayes
Author, speaker, educational consultant, and podcast host

Pete Cruz offers a fresh, unrestrained voice we don't see often in memoir. With stark vulnerability, *No Tears for Dad* provides a rare male perspective grappling with the forbidden feelings that arise from conflict of family and parental dynamics. The cross-cultural, cross-generational milieu enriches the texture, adroitly woven within a Christian context. This long-awaited book is now on the public shelves, much to the joy of all who have been mesmerized by author Pete Cruz reading aloud.

Kimberly Edwards
Author, *Sacramento Motorcycling: A Capital City Tradition*

There are too few books written about how and why God works to heal the hearts and minds of individuals. God intended no human should ever be without calm and inner peace. *No Tears for Dad* is a tale of anger and hurt stilled through God's ability to heal. The story proves God can restore anyone, at any age, in any circumstance—and for any reason—to a life of mental tranquility, forgiveness, and uncharacteristic love. Best of all, Pete Cruz tells his story with uncommon sensitivity and awareness.

Nora Profit
Executive Director, The Writing Loft

NO TEARS

FOR

Dad

PETE CRUZ

NO TEARS
FOR
Dad

MY PATH TO FORGIVENESS

FOREWORD BY CECIL MURPHEY, NEW YORK TIMES BESTSELLING AUTHOR

Published by Redemption Press,
PO Box 427, Enumclaw, WA 98022.
Toll-Free (844) 2REDEEM (273-3336)

Redemption Press is honored to present this title in partnership with the author. The views expressed or implied in this work are those of the author. Redemption Press provides our imprint seal representing design excellence, creative content, and high quality production.

Unless otherwise indicated, Scripture quotations are taken from the New King James version of the Bible.

Scripture quotations marked ESV are taken from the ESV® Bible (The Holy Bible, English Standard Version®), copyright © 2001 by Crossway, a publishing ministry of Good News Publishers. Used by permission. All rights reserved.

This memoir is a recollection of events whose time, place, and circumstances occurred as best I remember. I've endeavored to tell my story with transparency, self-reflection, and depth. It could be that someone else witnessing or experiencing the same occurrences as I may arrive at different viewpoints or conclusions. But life is according to one's own interpretations and perceptions. Some names have been changed to protect their privacy.

Printed in the United States of America

ISBN 13: 978-1-64645-823-3 (Paperback)
        978-1-64645-825-7 (ePub)
        978-1-64645-824-0 (Mobi)

LCCN: 2022909109

*Dedicated to the memory
of my sister, Mimi.
1963–2013
For her unfailing faith in me.
Taken too early by cancer.*

Contents

Foreword

Despite the fact that Pete Cruz tells about his painful childhood, it's not a woe-is-me book. It's uplifting and inspirational.

His words have an easy flow and are what we call written with heart. He enables us to feel his pain and the joy.

At first, I wasn't sure I wanted to read it. Like many others, I'd endured a painful childhood. My father was a functional alcoholic—he never missed a day of work or a weekend of drunkenness. And about once a week, his anger erupted on my baby brother and me. Verbal abuse was a regular part of his vocabulary—sober or drunk.

The worst and most insults were when he called us lazy warts. That never made sense to me, except that I knew warts didn't move or do anything. He meant I was lazy.

I carried most of those vile statements inside my head until my forties. By then I had earned two master's degrees, served as a missionary to Kenya for six years, and I'd published more than one hundred articles and two books.

One morning I rushed out of the shower crying, "I'm not lazy! I'm not lazy!"

Surprise covered my wife's face. "Whoever said you were?"

"My father did. Regularly."

My father was still alive when that happened. Shortly afterward, I sensed he was going to die soon, so I flew a thousand miles to see him. I sat across from him and said, "I always wanted your love and appreciation. I never got them." For perhaps twenty minutes I poured out my heart, all but begging Dad for a kind word.

"Well, all right," he said. Then he got out of his chair and walked into his bedroom. He closed the door, and I didn't see him again until the next morning when he waved goodbye.

I tell this because I was able to lovingly confront my father and talk to him without being knocked around. Pete Cruz never had that opportunity to talk to his father and challenge his constant abuse.

In reading Pete Cruz's *No Tears for Dad*, I realized his life was far worse than mine. Most of us have no idea what it's like to live in a house where we're verbally abused every day, and often physically as well. He was beaten again whenever he tried to respond to his father.

Worse than the verbal attacks, not once in Cruz's life did he ever hear a single word of affirmation or kindness from his father. Every day the message was, "You're worthless. You'll never amount to anything."

That's the negative side of the book. Cruz left home, graduated from college, and got an excellent job. He married and had a daughter. By normal standards, his life was successful. He took his wife and child to see his father. Even then, he heard, "You're worthless. You'll never amount to anything."

That was the last time Pete Cruz saw his father alive, but not the last of the harsh messages. But like many of us with painful childhoods, the hurtful messages were lodged deeply inside.

He and his wife divorced, and Cruz finally admitted he was expressing the anger of his father.

The beautiful part of this book is that after he met healthy men at a Bible study, Cruz slowly overcame his past and built a contented life.

That's the important part of the book—the changes he was able to make. And he writes vividly of the steps he took to stop being the victim.

After I finished reading his words, I smiled in contentment. Cruz had finally learned to love and accept himself as loveable and worthwhile.

Cecil Murphey is the author or co-author of 140 books, including *Gifted Hands* with Dr. Ben Carson and *90 Minutes in Heaven* with Don Piper.

Prologue

—————————————————

My youngest sister, Mimi, came on the line. "I'm sorry to tell you, but Dad died."

At 1:30 in the morning, her voice from the kitchen answering machine roused me from a dream.

I slumped back and stared at the ceiling. The words, "Ding-dong! The witch is dead," played in my head.

I had regularly visited Dad, driving unannounced from my home in Sacramento, California, to Milpitas, in the San Francisco Bay Area. I pretended I happened to be in the area. Our few conversations were tense and impersonal. He'd ask a question, and I answered in as few words as possible. Most of the time, his questioning felt like an interrogation. I rarely stayed more than an hour. When I drove away, it amazed me that he seemed pleased that I'd stopped by.

As I lay in bed, vivid memories replayed in my mind from the last time I'd seen him, more than a year earlier. His critical manner disappeared when he first saw his infant granddaughter, Natalia. He cradled her in his arms, cooing baby-talk and caressing her cheeks. It was so foreign. I hadn't witnessed his displaying affection with anyone before. Still, I perched like a hawk, ready to swoop should his unpredictable rage surface. He handed her back to my wife, Martina, and I sighed in relief.

While I stowed things in the truck for the drive back to Sacramento, Martina chatted with Mom in the garage.

"We're saving to buy a house. Pete works for the state now. He teaches classes for new supervisors."

Just as I shut the truck door, Dad came out of the house and approached my wife.

"Pete's no good!" His words carried little emotion. He looked right at me to make sure I listened. "Pete will never amount to anything."

We'd driven up in a new truck. My wife and I were both college graduates. We had a beautiful daughter. And I was a year into my job as the lead training officer in my state department.

"Get in the car," I said to my wife. "Now!" She walked to our truck while I turned to Mom. "I won't be back."

I expected her to say and do nothing as she always had. Instead, she dropped her head and mumbled, "I know."

She'd seen similar departures by my five older siblings. Each of us, at different times, had been yelled at: "When you turn eighteen, you can get the hell out of my house!" It pained me to see Mom realize that her son, the one who kept coming back, had finally had enough.

I shed no tears. I felt no sadness. All that had dried up decades ago when I stopped showing my feelings.

I struggled to accept that the father-son relationship I longed for would never happen. He never talked about his life in the Philippines or what it was like when he came to the United States or how he'd met Mom. He didn't talk about the jobs he'd held or his schooling. I only knew him as an angry man.

He hadn't attended my college graduation. Or my wedding. I yearned to share my educational and career accomplishments with him. I longed for him to know the person I had become. As an adult, I had moved on, but my heart ached for the boy inside me who never got a pat on the back— the boy who'd never be told, "I'm proud of you."

I shifted into reverse and backed out of the driveway for good.

That was the last time I saw my father.

―――

I dropped off my wife and daughter in Milpitas to stay with Mom while I met the others at the funeral home. Except for Pat, my oldest brother, and Mimi, my youngest sister, who stayed in the area, the rest of us scattered throughout the US. Though connections were limited to weddings and funerals, we still cared about each other.

Three siblings milled about toward the back of the mortuary.

Buster turned to me and asked, "What do you think Dad would say now?"

Scoop, another older brother, jumped in: "What a rebolting debelepment diss iss." One of our father's catch phrases, *What a revolting development this is*, came out that way with his heavy Filipino accent.

"I'm going to pok pok your head." I mimicked Dad's threats to stay in line.

"Isn't dat someting?" Buster scolded in perfect imitation of Dad.

Mimi laughed loudly. "You guys are too funny."

"Be quiet over there," Cookie, the oldest, blurted from the other side of the room. She snickered, unable to contain her amusement.

As we gathered with our three other siblings, the attendant asked, "Do you have any questions?"

"Are we there at the graveside when the coffin is lowered into the grave? What happens next?" Pat, the oldest brother, wanted to know.

"When the casket is lowered, you may place any mementos or sentimental items on it," the assistant said in her most understanding voice.

"For Pete, it's going to be rocks," Buster chuckled. "You're going to hear Bang! Clang! Boom!" He implied I got the worst of it growing up. My big brother also knew how to get me started.

"Ha, ha," I hooted. "No, you're going to hear rumbling behind you as I pull up with a bulldozer full of boulders." I raised my arms scoop-like. "They'll come crashing down . . ."

The rest of the family pursed their lips in an effort to maintain decorum. The attendant averted her eyes. Most families would be in a state of melancholy and grief.

We were not like most families.

The next afternoon, we gathered at Pat's house to relax and enjoy each other's company. I reviewed Dad's obituary in the *San Jose Mercury News*. His viewing was that evening.

"Anyone doing a eulogy?" I looked to Cookie.

"No . . ." Her answer hung in the air. It seemed to be the first time the topic had come up.

I deferred to Pat. "Nope. Not me." The expression on his face indicated one couldn't pay him enough.

"Anyone?" I received blank faces and turned-away eyes. "I guess I will."

Our dad was still the major influence in our lives. I couldn't let him go without saying something. I had a few hours to formulate a fitting send-off for the next day's funeral.

In the first-row pew of St. Justin Church, I reviewed my notes.

Father Davis stood with Pat below the pulpit, outlining the program. "Is anyone doing a eulogy?"

"Yeah, Pete." Pat nodded toward me.

The tall and lanky clergyman hurried to me, his dark robe swishing with each stride. He towered over me.

"If you're going to use this as a forum to disparage your father, here isn't the place," he stated in a tone reserved for catechism classes.

"No, it's not like that. That's not what I have in mind." I offered the priest a reassuring smile, which might've been mistaken for a grimace.

He said nothing else, then turned and walked away. I joined my family, who'd assembled in the second row on both sides of the center aisle.

While I waited for my cue, I paid little attention to the service. Delivering a speech in front of my family would be unlike any workshop I'd ever conducted. Here, I would lay open my heart and attempt to put the life of Fausto Elegado Cruz in proper perspective.

"Is there anyone here to give the eulogy?" Father Davis asked. I suspected he hoped I had reconsidered. He peered at me.

"I am." I rose to my feet.

With deliberate steps, I walked to the stage while my stomach fluttered like a shuffling deck of cards. My family didn't know what to expect. I was little brother to them. As the sixth of eight kids, I rarely did anything to draw attention.

While adjusting the microphone, I surveyed my family, their spouses, and others in attendance. Several rows back, I noted three of Mom's friends and one of Mimi's coworkers in another row. I glanced at Father

Prologue

Davis to the side, who was standing at strict attention. At the back wall, beyond rows of empty pews resembling untilted dominoes, leaned a mortuary attendant waiting to direct our dad's removal. In all, only nineteen people assembled for Dad's final exit.

The church loomed cavernously, and its emptiness accentuated its size. Up to this point, my family sat like impatient passengers waiting at a bus stop.

I took a deep breath.

"I'm certain we're all wondering where Dad is now. Is he viewing us from above, in heaven, or from a lesser place down below?" My family's eyes remained fixed on me.

"Putting it mildly, our dad was hard to live with. We didn't even know him. We were recipients of painful kicks from his combat boots. Was he in the army? The way he ordered us around says so. We've wondered if the discoloration below his one eye was the result of a powder burn. He came from the Philippines. What was life like for him there? Did he go to college? He seemed to be very educated. He spoke several languages. We've seen his penmanship. It's elegant, beautiful. And here we are, each of us successful because of him.

"In our beginnings in San Jose, we were poor farmworkers." My family kept rapt attention. "He landed us in a brand-new house in middle-class Milpitas. Although we were on welfare until Mom got a job, it was a much better life than working the fields. Where would we be if Dad hadn't gotten us out?"

My memory flashed back thirty years to our dilapidated house with no heating, working toilet, or shower.

"Despite Dad's severe behavior, he did things that showed he truly cared. How many times did we hear him recite the first exercise in beginning typing class, which contains all the letters of the alphabet: *The quick brown fox jumps over the lazy dog*? That's because he insisted we know how to type. Likewise, we know how to swim because he made us take lessons. He thought it was important for me, Scoop, and Buster to know how to skate. For weeks, we skated in circles in the garage as if we were in roller derby. I'm glad because I love to skate. When each of us reached age sixteen, he gave us a car."

My sisters' faces drooped, and tears flooded their eyes. Mom, usually distant and silent, bent over and gagged, trying to deny her welling-up emotions. She pulled a tissue from her purse and wiped her eyes.

The priest appeared less stiff and guarded. He stepped forward and continued to listen.

"Even with what he did for us, we still wonder if he loved us. He didn't show it. He never said anything about love to us. Most of the time he screamed at us, criticized us, beat us. Was he capable of love? I really didn't know until yesterday." I paused for a needed breath. "While we looked at caskets, Martina was at home with Mom."

I told them about Kiko, a young man who lived up the street. Martina was relaxing in the garage when Kiko drove up in his Jeep.

"Did Frank die?" he asked.

"Yes, he did."

"I thought so. I saw the ambulance." He had a tear in his eye and went on to say, "I loved him."

As I said those words aloud, my voice cracked and I turned from the pedestal. The word "love" had never been used in our family.

My sister's eyes gushed tears. Pat dabbed his eyes with a handkerchief, while Buster allowed his tears to flow.

To my astonishment, Scoop, the one we all agreed was the most like our dad, bawled uncontrollably. I recalled the intense shouting matches between him and Dad. My memory went back to when we were teenagers. Scoop writhed in pain on the floor while Dad whipped him with a belt more than a hundred times.

"My first summer home from college, I was in the garage when Kiko rode up on his bicycle. He must've been about seven, a cute little kid.

"'What're you doing?' he asked. A few days later, he rode up again and asked the same thing.

"It makes perfect sense to me that in all these years we've been away, Kiko visited Dad in the garage. I'm sure Dad befriended him, and I think Dad likely talked to him in ways he never did with us. Maybe that was a second chance for Dad to show he cared about someone, or that he was capable of love."

Prologue

The funeral attendant in the back took a step from the wall and beamed. I sensed this wasn't the usual sendoff he was used to hearing.

"Is Dad looking at us from above or looking at us from below? I'm going to bet it's from above. I believe when it's time for each of us to go, he'll be there with God, welcoming us home."

I returned to my seat. My sisters and Scoop continued to sob. Mom stared at her lap. Pat looked wistful, and Buster grinned at me with pride.

The funeral attendant took the stage, and in a gentle voice, provided interment directions. He stepped away from the mic, then turned back as if he'd changed his mind. He resumed: "Truly we have heard some things we all can take to heart. We are all moved by what has taken place today. Let us go on to ensure a proper burial and have something you can hold on to for the rest of your lives."

His words warmed my heart, and I thanked him after he stepped from the stage.

Father Davis approached me with ease in his steps. His eyes reflected softness, and he smiled with a demeanor much different than when we had first met. He asked me to visit when I came to the area. I assured him I would, but I knew it likely wouldn't happen.

I rejoined my family. They shed tears for Dad.

From me, there were none.

1

The Pits

Before the emergence of the Silicon Valley, an apple was a fruit and not a computer. In the late 1950s and, '60s, San Jose was an agricultural area.

Many people don't recall their infancy. But I do. Abandonment and neglect etched themselves into my psyche.

My family lived in a small, dilapidated farmhouse, secluded inside the orchards in east San Jose. Our nearest neighbors lived on the other side of the orchards.

In the summer months, my entire family left for the fields before daylight without me. Mom, or my oldest sister, Cookie, would check on me around lunchtime. They reached over the wood slats of my crib to hand me a warm bottle. They didn't say anything, nor did they hold me. After I finished, they took the bottle and walked away. Sometimes I cried. But no one heard me, and I eventually stopped crying. The next time I saw my family was at dinnertime.

Did my family really leave me for hours on end when I was young? Farm workers couldn't afford childcare and needed to work just to survive.

As an adult, similar situations trigger feelings of isolation. If I don't hear from a loved one in a reasonable time, intense anxiety clutches me. Dark rooms grip me in panic. Night lights occupy every room in my house, and too many flashlights and candles reside in drawers.

Each summer morning, I listened as my family stirred from their beds and put on work clothes and shoes to leave for the fields. Waxed paper being torn from its box and folded over homemade sandwiches alerted me that activities were in full swing. Bag lunches and filled thermoses completed the preparations.

Shuffling feet paused at the kitchen door. The screen door slammed with a sharp bang. Our station wagon's tires crunched over the gravel driveway, transporting them away. In the distance, the sound of our car faded into the stark silence that surrounded me. Abandoned for another day, I pulled the covers over my head, afraid of the dark, and I tried to go back to sleep.

When I was a bit older, I mustered the courage to plead with Dad: "Can I go work outside with everyone?" I chanced his anger, but fears of staying at home by myself pushed me to ask again.

"You're too young," was his usual reply.

But one day he looked closer at me, perhaps deciding if I was going to be a help or a hindrance.

With clenched fingers, I braced for another refusal. I'd seen him yell at others for asking questions.

"Okay," he said in a surprisingly calm voice. "We'll give you a try."

The next morning, sleep pressed upon me as my family readied to leave for the fields. Fear of isolation pulled me wide awake. If I didn't meet them at the kitchen door, they'd leave without me.

I rose from my bed and gazed out the window. Outside was devoid of light. My stomach jolted from memories of all the mornings overcome by haunting darkness. I hurried to put on my clothes, scared I'd be left behind. I ran to meet the others in the kitchen.

Dad drove to a nearby orchard. On the way, no one said anything. The early morning muted everyone.

The drive was unremarkable on the paved roads, until Dad braked and swerved onto a dirt road. The ride got bumpier and louder. Clouds of dust swirled beside the car, and rocks rattled its underside. The tires shuddered to a stop at our destination.

The cool morning air brushed against me as I got out of the car. Before rows of trees, I stood in the dark. No one said a word.

The Pits

I followed Dad to a tree where a wooden ladder had already been put into place. A gray aluminum bucket hung empty, its handle hooked inside a higher rung. Dad motioned to me to climb up. Once I got high enough, he told me to stop and pick the cherries within reach. After observing me a short time, he left. I guessed he went to check on the other family members.

After a while he came back, the foreman with him. Dad peered inside my pail and grabbed a handful.

"Good," he said. "You picked the ripe ones." My heart warmed with pride. I couldn't remember his ever saying I did something good. I looked forward to picking more.

Dad turned to the foreman for confirmation, and the foreman said something I couldn't hear.

Dad turned back to me. "You left the stems on the tree."

My heart sank. *I had failed.* I was scared he'd shake the ladder to make me come down. But instead, he said, "From now on, leave the stems on the cherries. That's good it doesn't bother you to climb that high, so keep at it."

I never told him the truth. Heights frightened me. But being left alone at home scared me more.

After the first day in the hot, dusty, and dirty orchards, I struggled to get out of bed. I regretted asking Dad if I could join the family. The work was hard and lasted from sunup to sundown. I hated getting up so early, but it was better than isolation at home.

Each bucket of cherries I picked was the pits.

2

Fowl Fears

I don't remember why we didn't continue to work in the fields. Maybe because we were receiving welfare benefits.

At the end of summer, my older brothers and sisters went to school. Because I wouldn't turn six until December of the following year, I had to wait for the next fall before beginning kindergarten.

During the school year, I was left to work in the yard. Mom did household chores and cared for my little brother, Perry, who was two years old.

I followed Dad around the farm. He'd tell me to do things like carry pieces of wood, get the hammer, hold the end of the tape measure, and hand him different tools.

I learned to obey his instructions exactly, or he exploded over the slightest miscommunication. If I didn't understand his directions the first time, and either performed the task wrong or had to ask for clarification, he made a big deal out of it. "Isn't that something?" he yelled at me or my siblings. "You can't even wash the pots the right way." He expected the copper bottoms to shine like a new penny.

Usually, I liked going with Dad on errands because it was a break from chores. The car rides let me relax so I could gaze out the window at the scenery.

When our chickens didn't lay enough eggs, we went to Olivera Egg Ranch in the east San Jose foothills.

The bright yellow company sign atop a high pole tickled me because it included a cartoon picture of a smiling egg with playful, happy eyes and a fancy bow tie.

After opening the car door, I wrinkled my nose from the sulfuric odor of chicken poop. We walked to the small store in front of the ranch where we could hear the birds' raucous cackling in the back areas. Inside the shop, refrigerated air made me shiver.

Dad picked up and carried two flats of eggs and two loaves of bread to the front counter. I followed behind with two cartons of milk. The young female clerk smiled and punched numbers on the cash register. She asked Dad something about the food stamps he had removed from his jacket. My father said something back. The clerk didn't understand what he said and repeated her question. Dad's thick Filipino accent must have bewildered her.

When he repeated his answer, her expression remained confused.

"What! You don't understand English? Oh, for Chrissakes!" Dad exploded. His rage always combined *Christ's sake* into one word. When Dad screamed that word, I cowered.

I glanced around, thankful no one else was in the store. My throat tightened, and I wanted to run back to the car.

The clerk's face flushed crimson. She avoided eye contact with Dad, and her hands trembled while making change.

Dad snatched the bills and coins from the counter and stuffed them in his pockets. He shook his head sideways in disgust, grabbed the eggs and bread, and stomped away.

Dad glared out the windshield the entire ride home.

I moved closer to the door, trying to make myself invisible.

That day I learned that routine public errands carried the same potential for worry and shame as it did at home. I walked on eggshells no matter where we went.

In the Cruz household, the chickens came before the eggs. That meant one of my main duties was to feed the chickens. They lived in a makeshift coop with walls constructed of one-inch beanpoles that pointed skyward. It caged about a dozen hens and one enormous rooster. The birds perched on plywood shelves that ran alongside the slatted walls like kitchen counters. On the front of their roost, a narrow trough contained their feed.

Each morning, Dad led me through the kitchen door. I carried an aluminum pot half-filled with swill. I avoided looking at the slop and didn't know its ingredients. Often it appeared to be a slimy brown or gray vomit-like composition.

The chickens bobbed their heads in frenzy when they saw us near the coop. Amid their noisy squawks, I steeled myself for the job I was about to do.

Dad unwound a wire to open the narrow beanpole door. After I stepped inside by myself, he shut the door behind me, rewound the wire, and watched me feed the chickens.

My presence incited the birds to a shrieking crescendo. Each bird screeched in my face. I breathed through my mouth because of the caustic odor of chicken feces.

I eyed the monster rooster in the back corner, and he seemed to glare back at me. He was king, and I had trespassed into his domain. His head swerved side-to-side as if he was considering his attack.

I poured the swill-pot contents along the trough's path. My quivering hands helped the feed fall easily from the container. Fear of the chickens pushed me to do it too fast, and fear of Dad made me dispense the feed evenly so there'd be enough left to reach the end.

As I reached the opposite corner from where the rooster squatted, he lifted his massive avian body to stand. He screeched what sounded like a battle cry.

Terror clawed at me. I felt I was his enemy, his prey. He squawked in increasing volume and flew at me. I heard the helicopter beat of his flapping wings and felt the air around me displace as he soared, talons outstretched. I braced myself and turned away fast enough to take the penetrating pain of talons on my back.

Sometimes I couldn't help but release an audible gasp. But if I showed any objection, Dad might scream at me, open the door to wallop me, and leave me locked inside the coop.

Each day Dad witnessed an aerial assault on his son. Each day he stood outside the coop motionless, nothing more than a faceless statue.

Once I finished, he said nothing. He opened the door, let me out, and rewrapped the wire to secure the door.

I marched behind him into the house, the empty pot swiping against my leg.

Please don't make me go in there again, I wanted to cry out, but never did.

I feared my dad more than the giant rooster.

3

The Nightmare of Reality

Our small farmhouse was located in the vicinity of the San Jose Airport. Our nearest neighbors lived beyond many rows of apricot trees. Throughout the day, airplanes flew overhead, but I rarely bothered to look skyward because of their commonplace occurrence.

Late at night, I became aware of the airplanes when the drone of their small engines disrupted my sleep.

Recurring nightmares of my family and me at the airport plagued me. In the dream, I walked with them through the parking lot, but fell behind because my legs were too short to keep up. No matter how hard I tried, the distance between us increased. Making it worse, concrete parking blocks impeded my path. I stumbled over them because they were too high for my short legs to step over.

"Wait!" I shouted. In the slow way people move in dreams, Cookie turned to look back at me. She motioned to me to hurry up before she rejoined the group's deliberate march away.

Overhead, the sound of an airplane's droning dominated the landscape. Its relentless hum drowned out my screams.

My dream crumbled into a terrible nightmare of one-word shrieks. "Wait! Wait!" I mouthed slow-motion, unheard pleas.

Then my family disappeared from view among the rows of parked cars.

They've abandoned me forever.
I stared at the small pebbles dotting the asphalt lot.
Alone. I cried.

In the middle of the night, I flailed in bed and wrestled with my recurring nightmare of being left behind. Moans of anguish and agony poured forth as tears streamed from my eyes. I wanted to stop crying, but couldn't. My body shuddered as I huddled under my blankets.

I slept in the living room with my two older brothers, Buster and Scoop, our beds sat directly across from our parents' bedroom. In their room, the ceiling light consisted of a single unadorned light bulb hung by its electrical cord on a bent nail. If Dad turned on the light, that meant we were making noise, and he'd be furious.

Without warning, my bed covers were ripped away.

"Stop it!" my father roared. "What's wrong with you?"

Nothing was wrong with me except I couldn't stop my tears.

"Stop crying!"

His swinging open hand connected with my temple and spun my head sideways into the pillow.

He stomped back to his bedroom.

The stinging pain didn't compare to the shock and sorrow of being left alone and uncared for.

The cold night surrounded me.

Dad's bedroom light went off and darkness enclosed our house again.

I sat up to search for my bedsheets and found them crumpled on the floor. My insides felt the same.

I lay back down, turned to one side, and pulled the covers over my head. I cried silent, muffled sobs beneath my covers.

Every night I listened to the airplanes flying toward the airport, waiting for the drone to ebb in the distance—too afraid to fall asleep into another nightmare.

4

Kindergarten

—————————————•————————————

The Noble Elementary School buildings reminded me of where Mom brought me for doctor and dentist appointments. The light blue doors were numbered. There wasn't anyone around. It was quiet.

I followed her to one of the big doors, but was scared of what could be on the other side. She knocked, and out stepped a tall woman who peered at me from behind sharp-cornered glasses. She looked like a big owl, and her expression seemed to say, "Who is this?"

"I'm Mrs. Slater. Is this Pacifico?"

I was confused. That was the first time anyone had called me that name. My family always called me Peewee. I hated the name Peewee. It made me feel small, puny, and insignificant. When teased, a helpless feeling overwhelmed me, while shame threatened to burn a hole in my chest.

"You'll be leaving him with us until noon?"

Mom nodded.

Fear overwhelmed me. She could have said forever since I didn't know what noon meant. No one told me I was going to be there by myself.

My nightmare was coming true. *I'm really going to be abandoned.* I wailed loud and hard.

"It's okay, Pacifico. You'll have a lot of friends in here."

I didn't have friends at home, so I became even more afraid.

Mom looked at me without expression. She didn't seem to care.

I cried in full volume.

"Everything's going to be all right," Mrs. Slater said. She stooped to put her hand on my shoulder, and she looked at me with kindness.

Mom continued to observe my teacher and me. No emotion registered. Her face looked as if she were watching TV.

My teacher attempted to give me another assuring smile. "Your mother will be back to pick you up later." She turned to Mom and said, "I'll take it from here."

What could be behind the door terrified me. I shrieked even more.

Without a word, Mom turned and walked away.

I screamed louder. Just like in my nightmare, my family had walked away and never looked back.

Memories transported me to my crib. I saw the same thing—Mom leaving without saying anything. I wondered if she were coming back.

Realizing my bawling wasn't going to make her return, I stopped crying. I stared at the ground, sniffling.

Mrs. Slater escorted me through the door.

My new classmates viewed me curiously but said nothing. They were small like I was, and they didn't seem to mind that I cried. I wondered if they had cried too.

Later that day, one of my classmates showed me how to make airplanes out of clay. I smiled and held one on my fingers, flying it through the classroom sky. I knew how to make the droning sounds too.

I never got to play or use my imagination much at home.

From then on, I liked going to school, and Mrs. Slater was nice all the time. During the year, we finger-painted—one of my favorite activities. The squiggly lines I traced on my paper fascinated me.

When someone had a birthday, she brought that person a slice of birthday cake, and we sang "Happy Birthday." I learned it was a special day for our classmate, and only he or she got cake.

Toward the end of the year, she announced, "It's Pacifico's birthday!" and gave me the same triangle-shaped object wrapped in foil like those she had given other classmates. I was shocked. Only then did I realize that I, too, had a birthday.

"Happy birthday, dear Pacifico . . ." my class sang in unison. I wondered if Mrs. Slater might realize I didn't really have a birthday and would take the cake back.

At home, no one ever gave me cake or sang "Happy Birthday." In the years that followed, my special day went unnoticed. What should have been a happy day turned out to be annual heartbreak. I was tormented by the thought that no one seemed to care about the day I was born. Each year, a gaping wound reopened. *Am I a worthy person? Does anyone care about me?*

The first birthday party ever in my honor was a dinner given by a college campus organization of which I was a member.

In the family photo album, I saw that my sisters apparently had birthdays. They wore birthday dresses and ate cake and ice cream. But my other brothers didn't have birthday parties either, nor did I see photos of their birthdays.

I do remember my older sister Penny's sweet sixteen birthday party in December—the same month as mine. All day I helped Dad set up the garage. My sister got a new hi-fi record player. I was ten at the time. *Didn't I ever deserve anything?*

On one birthday, after I came home from junior high school, Dad addressed me as he usually did. "Change out of your school clothes so you can do chores."

Sadness draped over me. I walked to my room. *For my birthday, I get to work in the backyard.* My chest tightened and my breathing became shallow. It seemed like all I was good for was to do chores. I wanted to cry, but couldn't.

As a teenager, I cut school on my birthdays. I wanted to make my day special, so I wandered around by myself, bored and unhappy, hoping I wouldn't get caught for truancy.

One time Dad told me the school called. "Why didn't you go to school?"

Because it's my birthday! Doesn't anyone care? I wanted to yell. But I shrugged and walked to my room, thankful he didn't chase me for more of an answer.

As an adult working full time, I took my birthdays off.

Those days off were small gestures I used to salvage my self-esteem and acknowledge that I mattered—an attempt to do something for myself when no one else did anything for me. Yet most of the time on my birthdays, I wrestled with feeling empty, insignificant, and forgotten.

Nonetheless, I will never forget that birthday in kindergarten.

It was the day I turned six.

5

Missing Perry

—————————————————

"**He stopped breathing!**" Cookie wailed. Disbelief sent a torrent of tears streaming down her face.

Mom hunched over the kitchen counter and sobbed.

That January I was a little over seven years old. Perry was three.

At first, I wondered if my brother, Perry, was still in the car. But when Cookie said he stopped breathing, I knew he wasn't coming back.

Memories of him are fleeting, like a filmstrip with scenes, worn and cracked, catching within the projector's spool.

As kids, we had playfully rolled around on the floor.

He tagged along with me on our farm property. Other times, I kept an eye on him and followed. He was inquisitive and loved to explore and touch the agricultural equipment that lay about.

Some implements sat unused and rusted after seasons of rain. A few times I watched him lick rust—once an old stove propped against the barn wall, another time, a large, round blade on a disk plow that was completely rusted.

Pat caught him a few times and told him to stop.

I wondered if it would taste good to me, but I never tried it. In later years, I thought maybe he suffered from an iron deficiency.

After the day he died, my parents never mentioned him again. His photos disappeared. There was no funeral. I didn't know why.

Not long after he passed, I attended a religious service with Mom. I looked around at everyone, none of whom I or Mom knew. I expected the priest to say Perry's name, but he never did. I believed the service was for my brother, but it wasn't. It was just wishful thinking.

When we'd all reached adulthood, my brothers and sisters spoke of him. But rarely.

I missed him.

Where is he? Why doesn't anyone talk about him?

I pondered, grieved, and longed to know what happened.

As the years went on, I finished school, set about a career, and married. I never forgot about my little brother.

Through the years, I had asked Mom, "Where's Perry buried?"

"I don't know," she replied. Her face revealed nothing. I don't know how much she may have been in denial, but I didn't believe her.

I kept Perry in my heart and mind and vowed to search for him someday.

I was his big brother, and he was my little brother. We bonded as boys.

Thirty years later, I found where he was buried. The death certificate said he died of an unknown blood disorder.

6

The Unsafe Way

During the summer before my second-grade school year, we moved to Milpitas, a suburb of San Jose. Dad knew someone who bought the house as an investment. We could live there as long as we paid the $163.00 monthly mortgage.

Our move to a middle-class neighborhood was a significant event. We escaped poverty.

In San Jose, our dilapidated, desolate farmhouse sat amid orchards in complete darkness, except for occasional moonlight. It had two small bedrooms, a bathtub without a shower, peeling wallpaper, and yellowed, warped window shades. One time a piece of ceiling plaster splashed on Buster's plate at dinnertime.

Our toilet didn't work. During the day, we used an outhouse by the barn. In the evening, we used a bucket next to the broken toilet.

Because of our large family, by the next morning, the white porcelain pail with a red-painted rim brimmed with excrement and urine. My assignment was to dump it at the base of a fig tree each day.

In our new neighborhood, it wasn't completely dark at night, and we weren't isolated. Neighbors lived up and down the street, and streetlamps stood in front of every other house.

I roomed with Buster and Scoop. We slept on top of our hospital-issued, creaky folding beds brought from San Jose. In the new house, our bedroom window faced the backyard and had white, aluminum venetian blinds. In the evening, muffled light from a streetlamp on the road behind us shined through the slats, providing reassuring lighting. I no longer needed to fear the dark.

———

One Saturday, my two brothers and I rode our bicycles to the corner of Calaveras Boulevard and Park Victoria Drive to watch a sign go up for the new Safeway supermarket. We sat on our bikes, our faces skyward, gazing at a big, long crane that held a gigantic red *S* in position. The red *S*, encircled in white, shone bright against the clear blue sky.

The crane looked like an erector set come alive. I gripped my handlebars with excited anticipation. Occasionally, I glanced at the store building, not yet open, curious about what made it *safe* and why it didn't look like a *way*.

After Safeway opened, Dad frequently sent me on my bicycle to buy things. Sometimes I went only to buy a can of evaporated milk.

After I got home, I handed the small, brown grocery bag to Dad for inspection. He emptied the bag to see if the contents were precisely as ordered. Then I pulled dollar bills, coins, and a receipt from my pants pocket and put them on the kitchen table.

I stood motionless, awaiting his verdict.

"You got the wrong change!" He glared at me as if I'd kicked a dog. He turned to face whoever else occupied the kitchen area and shouted God's name in vain. His face intense, he stepped toward me and thrust the coins, bills, and receipt into my hand. "Go back and get it!"

Only seven years old, I didn't know how to make change. Maybe if I brought a pencil and paper with me, I could figure it out, but I worried I'd get yelled at if I took too long to get home. Every time, I hoped the store clerks gave me correct change.

When I walked back into Safeway, I found the same cashier. I dreaded I might be in trouble with him too. An urge to cry pushed against my face. "My dad says I got the wrong change."

"Oh, I'm sorry." The clerk smiled while he reviewed the receipt and money. "Here," he said. Relief spread over me. My breathing became normal when he handed me additional change.

After I rode home, Dad took the money and receipt I laid on the kitchen table and counted the change. When he said nothing, I walked to the living room, relieved to sit down.

"Can you imagine? Peewee got the wrong change." His voice always rose when he criticized. He directed comments to Cookie at the sink, where she washed dishes. He clucked his tongue and shook his head.

Ashamed, I stared at the laces in my shoes. Voices from the TV echoed without meaning.

A few days later, I went through the kitchen after finishing backyard chores. I walked by Dad and Penny, who were at the stove cooking dinner. I rested on the living room sofa. "Can you imagine? The other day, Peewee got the wrong change." He followed his criticism with curse words.

His continual rehashing of the same offense cemented the idea that I couldn't do anything right. I needed to be perfect if I wanted him to stop his harsh criticisms.

During another Safeway errand, the cashier didn't give me a receipt. Cold realization overtook me as I stepped on the black mat that automatically opened the exit. I was always afraid to question any adult, thinking they might have the same temper as Dad.

I got the courage to explain, but the clerk looked through her rolls of receipts and couldn't find it.

My heart pounded and my stomach churned as I slowly rode home, worrying what form of punishment awaited.

"She couldn't find it." I braced myself for the tidal wave.

He hollered Christ's name in vain and behaved as if I had hurled a rock through the front window. His use of the Lord's name sometimes signaled a forthcoming belt lashing. Other times, he walked away. I didn't know what to expect.

A few weeks later, I went into the living room after finishing chores outside. I sat down in the armchair by the window and peered at the occasional passing car. I heard the kitchen sink faucet as Pat washed his hands after working in the garage.

"Peewee didn't get a receipt. Isn't that something?" Dad said to my oldest brother.

With Dad, when I thought it was safe, it never was. His mental and emotional condemnations were more hurtful than the physical beatings. Safeway was always a danger way to me.

7

Untethered

Second grade at my new school in Milpitas, Alexander Rose Elementary School, began the same way it had in kindergarten. I bawled nonstop, again terrified of being left with strangers.

After a while, I got tired of crying, and I stared at the ground. My new teacher, Mrs. Yoshida, led me inside and escorted me to an empty seat. My classmates looked bigger than what I remembered in San Jose. They sat at their desks, unconcerned about what had happened outside.

Every day during recess, I sat against a chain link fence with narrow slats of wood woven through each link. The fence separated the school buildings from the playground area. While most of the kids played on the monkey bars, merry-go-round, and swings, I liked to sit away from everybody because I was afraid no one liked me.

I sat and faced the ground, alone with my thoughts. I daydreamed about Mr. Wizard, a cartoon lizard. He sent his young friend, Tooter the Turtle, to different places in time. "Help me, Mr. Wizard! Help me!" Tooter shouted when he got himself into trouble. Mr. Wizard wore a sorcerer's robe, cone hat, and spectacles. Each time he rescued Tooter, he waved his wand and said the magic words, "Twizzle, twazzle, twozzle, twome, time for this one to come home."

At school and home, I wanted Mr. Wizard to help me.

"What are you doing?" Someone's voice interrupted my daydream.

Startled, I opened my eyes and looked up.

"What are you doing?" Penny said again. My junior-high sister walked by whenever she had early dismissal. This time, she stopped and stooped over me, her eyes wide open, wanting an answer. "Why aren't you playing with the other kids?"

I shrugged and didn't know what to say.

"I always see you sitting by yourself. You should play with the other kids."

"I don't know," was all I could answer.

She turned and walked away.

When I saw my classmates having fun, I didn't know how to ask if I could join them. I was too scared to play with others.

Most afternoons, the sun shone through the narrow slats of the fence that gave me support, shade, and security. The sounds of recess faded from my attention. My head down, the flat, gray playground cement completely occupied my vision. I stopped looking at the playing kids and shut the world out.

"Pacifico, do you want to play tetherball?" A voice startled me.

Linda, my classmate, stood between me and an empty tetherball circle. I didn't know what to do, but her face suggested disappointment if I didn't get up.

"I'll show you how."

"Okay." I got up and followed her to the waiting tetherball.

She smacked the ball to make it and the attached rope wrap itself around the pole. She told me to hit the tetherball back the other way so it wouldn't wind all the way around or she would win. It fascinated me to see the rope twisting around the pole and the ball go round and round until it came to a sudden bobbing stop when it hit the pole.

In the days following, I trailed Linda out to the tetherball poles. When others wanted to play, we took turns, or I waited my turn by standing outside the painted circle.

In time, I felt secure enough to play at other parts of the playground. I enjoyed swinging on the monkey bars, and my favorite game was kickball.

Having friends from class to play with made recess fun.

Untethered

During an assembly at the end of the school year, the principal announced that for the first time ever, awards would be given to the boy and girl in each class who demonstrated good citizenship. My teacher, Mrs. Yoshida, stood on stage with other teachers.

After the first-grade awards, Mrs. Yoshida walked to the microphone and announced, "For the second grade, our good citizens are Linda Knight . . ." I glanced down the row and watched Linda get up from her seat. ". . . and Pacifico Cruz."

I looked at Mrs. Yoshida, but stayed seated. I didn't believe she had called my name. She stared at me and nodded slightly. I jumped off my chair and hurried to Linda before she went up the steps.

On stage, I turned to face the audience. Mrs. Yoshida handed us each a red pennant that read "Good Citizenship Award" in large felt letters.

Linda deserved the award because she was a good citizen. And she befriended me by getting me to leave the fence to play tetherball. From then on, I gained the confidence to join others and discovered that the other kids liked playing with me. It seems that I also won the award, in part because of my shyness. I always sat quietly in class and did what the teacher asked.

When I returned to my seat, my classmates smiled. The award showed I was valued and deserving of recognition. It meant I was a good student and able to get along with others.

My good citizenship award was the first of many views from people, other than Dad, declaring me worthwhile.

I started to believe that maybe I wasn't as worthless as Dad claimed.

8

Comic Book Relief

A **loud thumping noise** blared from Dad's bedroom window. In the backyard, we turned our heads and saw him banging on the window with his fist. The windowpane vibrated back and forth like a diaphragm in a stereo speaker. I stood frozen, half expecting glass shards to crash outward.

My brothers also looked paralyzed. Dad cursed us for horsing around instead of working. Scoop had shoved me to the ground, and Buster taunted me.

Dad dashed from view and in seconds bounded from the side of the house like an attacking wolverine. I usually wanted to be first on his hit list to get it over with because watching my brothers get thrashed seemed to make my turn more painful.

Dad's explosive behavior occurred often. I wished he could've just said, "Stop it, you guys! Get back to work." I think we would have. Or if he had asked, "What's going on? What are you fighting about?" maybe it would have calmed the situation. Just once, I wanted him to protect me and say, "Quit picking on your little brother. He didn't do anything to you."

Instead, his all-consuming rage lashed out every time. He never allowed protest, excuse, or explanation. His lack of patience and understanding made a bad situation worse.

I toiled in the side yard, intent at unearthing a stubborn weed with my hoe. The temperature was cool, and the Saturday morning sun cast a shaft of light between my house and the neighbor's.

"Hey, Peewee!"

I glanced to the side, expecting to see Dad.

"Over here."

I looked toward the front.

"No, over here. It's me, Ritchie." My next-door neighbor, Ritchie, stood at his garage. He gazed at me from behind thick, black-framed glasses. I was a third grader and he was in sixth. "Do you want to look at some comic books?"

"What're those?"

"Come over and I'll show you."

After propping the hoe against the house, I hurried to Ritchie's garage. I swerved my head back and forth like an owl to keep an eye out for Dad. My ears remained keen for his hollering, which would have me sprinting back home if he discovered I had abandoned my post.

Ritchie dragged a large cardboard box along the garage floor, its flaps open. I peered inside to see it full of comic books. He pushed his glasses to the bridge of his nose and grabbed a stack in both hands. On a clear space on the workbench, he laid them out. "I have *Spider-Man, Superman, Fantastic Four, The Incredible Hulk, Archie, Richie Rich.*"

The vivid color and glossy artwork of the covers captivated me.

"I have to get back to work." I feared Dad could erupt any second. "Can I come back later and look at them?"

"Sure, they'll be here. Just knock on my door."

I returned to the side yard and resumed ridding our yard of weeds, but remained lost in thought about comic books. They looked similar to Sunday morning comic strips, but more exciting.

After working all morning, I gulped down lunch and knocked on Ritchie's front door. He opened it and led me through his house to the garage.

Each page of the comic books came under review. I inspected them as if they were maps to pirates' hidden treasures. Within each page, battles between superheroes and supervillains unfolded. Drawings depicted heroes protecting cities or going on adventures to other planets.

I peppered Ritchie with questions about the various characters. What's an Avenger? How did Spider-Man get his powers? Why does Batman wear a mask?

"You can take some home and read them," Ritchie offered. "When you're done, come back and get more."

At home I lay in bed and read about other times, places, and worlds. Some heroes flew through the air, some had superstrength, while others unleashed beams of energy from their hands or eyes. Comic book heroes fought for justice. In each story, the good guys always won.

Batman emerged as my favorite. He didn't have superpowers, but relied on his mind and physical fitness. Like me, he believed he lived in an unfair world, and his outlook was grim, serious, and angry. He wore a mask to hide his identity, and he struck fear into the bad guys.

In a short time, I read all of Ritchie's comics and began my own collection.

Each month, I rode my bicycle to Rexall Drug Store, which was a few blocks from Safeway. The comic book carousel squeaked when I turned it as I searched for titles such as *Batman, Detective Comics starring Batman and Robin,* and *The Amazing Spider-Man.*

Though a few cost ten cents, most were twelve. I bought them using money from my paper route. Dad kept my earnings, but I never told him about the tips my customers gave me when I collected subscription fees each month.

My brothers enjoyed comic books too. On occasion, we'd go with Dad to the San Jose Flea Market. We walked through the aisles, our eyes focused on locating stacks of once-read comic books among used clothing and housewares. A private seller might sell comic books at three for ten cents or less.

Unseen by Dad, we amassed a large comic book collection in our bedroom. And each night before sleeping, I escaped the real world through those comic books.

9

Belt Buckled

"**Hey, Pacifico,**" my school friend Guy asked. "You want to come over to my house after school? We could play baseball with my brothers."

I smiled. In third grade, Guy had become one of my best friends, and I was happy he wanted to hang around with me after school.

"Okay. I'll finish my paper route, and unless my dad wants me to do anything after that, I'll be over."

After school I delivered newspapers on my bicycle. It was a cool, fall afternoon as I focused on completing my route. I glided in and out of driveways as the canvas bag attached to my handlebars swung back and forth. I bicycled up walkways and tossed each paper on the porch or doormat, then made my way as fast as I could to the next house.

After finishing my route, I rode home and parked in the garage. Before entering the house, I noticed an empty laundry basket in front of our washing machine. When I opened the lid, warmth from a just completed spin cycle brushed my face.

On entering the kitchen, Dad looked at me and said, "Go and dry the laundry."

We didn't own a clothes dryer. In cold weather, we dried clothes indoors. A clothesline ran between the kitchen and living room. We hung the wash on clothes hangers and used a wooden pole to hoist the hangers onto nails hammered into the ceiling beams above the hallway.

I jumped to my task, not pausing for a breather until the laundry basket was half full. I hoped a simple okay from Dad signaled release to visit my friend, Guy.

"After you're done hanging the clothes, go to the backyard and pick rocks."

My heart sank as if it were chained to a stone and tossed into the sea. I wouldn't be going to my friend's house. After picking rocks from the dirt pile, manure was mixed with the mound of earth to fertilize the garden. Most of the time, picking rocks seemed like a chore whose only purpose was to keep me busy.

Dad sat at the kitchen table and watched me.

The remaining clothes in the basket seemed heavier. The pole became cumbersome and the ceiling beams looked higher.

I couldn't hide my disappointment, even with my back to him.

"What! You don't like that?" Dad boomed. My eyes widened as I turned to stare at him. My body tensed, awaiting explosion. His searing eyes locked onto mine, and I cowered behind the laundry basket. Now he was going to add sorrow to my disappointment.

He sprang from his chair and stomped to me. I braced myself, expecting him to take a swing or kick at me. Instead, he moved his head side-to-side, like a lion seeking to devour his prey. In an instant, he sprinted to his bedroom.

Inside his bedroom closet three belts hung on separate nails. One leather belt was thin, long, and narrow. Another leather belt was medium width. And the third was a thick, fabric Boy Scout belt with a large, brass buckle.

I feared the thin belt most. It lashed like a whip and stung on impact. Its narrow width cut the skin. In previous incidences when fending off the thin belt with my arms or by turning my back, the whip-like effect lacerated my cheeks or neck.

The belt I minded least was the one normally worn by Boy Scouts. Although I never got to join the Scouts, Dad must've bought it from the thrift store where we sometimes shopped for clothes. The belt was thick and wide. I preferred it because it wasn't made of leather. On impact it didn't tear or sting. I could weather its heavier blows easier.

There was no choice but to stay still. My breathing slowed and my stomach constricted. I glanced toward the street through our living room window, knowing if I ran, there was nowhere to go, and when I came back, the punishment would be far worse.

I returned a damp shirt to the basket. My arms drooped at my sides to await the coming storm.

His face contorted like a snarling dog. His eyes glazed over in fury and he wielded the Boy Scout belt. At first, I was slightly relieved because this belt didn't sting like the others. Then I realized he had grasped its other end. The large, metal buckle flew at me. I turned my back and registered pain upon my torso as he cursed me. I twisted my body and maneuvered my shoulders and arms at different angles to minimize the belt's distance and impact as much as possible.

Though I successfully evaded major harm, the final blow looped at me at such an angle that I could only nod my head forward. The buckle crashed against the back of my skull. I felt a pinch and a tearing sensation.

Then Dad walked away to his room.

I reached for the back of my head. Cut flesh mixed with blood and hair. When I pulled my fingers away, they dripped red. I expected to feel warm liquid flow to my neck, but found solace when it didn't. The hair on the back of my head must've stemmed the flow. I stopped myself from crying because it would only invite additional assault.

No one was around. My older brothers and sisters participated in after-school activities. As the youngest boy, I learned that my role was to work at home.

I didn't know where Mom was. Normally, she'd be preparing dinner in the kitchen. Nonetheless, she'd never stopped Dad's attacks before. I'd long learned that I couldn't count on her to protect me.

After hanging the clothes, I went to the backyard to pick up rocks. Our backyard fence blocked the late afternoon sun, and I squatted over mounds of dirt in the cold gloom. I resisted the temptation to touch my head because my hands were dirty from reaching into the piles for rocks. *How big is the cut?*

At the dinner table, Dad never sat with us. He stayed in his room, but told us we couldn't talk. That night I looked at my plate sullenly, finished quickly, and then retreated to my room. The optimism of visiting Guy had dissolved into an ugly, mangled rage.

I sat in my room trying to read a comic book, but my thoughts swirled. *What do I do about the mass of dried blood on the back of my head?*

That night I did my best to sleep on my stomach. I tossed about while I lay face down, turning my head to either side. I didn't want to lay the back of my head on my pillow in case the wound reopened. I imagined the cut a gaping chasm making a mess of my pillow, and I worried I'd get into trouble if it did.

Thoughts of how I was going to hide this from my classmates made for a sleepless night.

10

Haircut

Mrs. Proven usually smiled when she called on me because I knew the answers to most of her questions. I never raised my hand to ask questions because at home I had learned to not volunteer my opinion. I was well-behaved and didn't do anything to interrupt the class. I considered myself the teacher's pet, though no one ever said so.

The next day in school, the dried blood on the back of my head made it hard to pay attention.

In Mrs. Proven's class, we sat where we wanted, so I sat in the back row to keep everyone in front of me. I worried someone would point out the blood on my head. I always told the truth, which meant I'd have to say my dad belted me. If the principal called Dad, I'd be in really big trouble.

Twice during the day, my teacher walked to the back of the room. I turned toward her, pretending to follow where she was going, but I just wanted to keep her from seeing the back of my head.

During recess, I positioned myself against a wall.

"Maybe this Saturday you can come over." Guy followed up with me since I didn't get to go over to his house the day before.

"Yeah," I replied, "maybe after I finish my chores in the morning."

I remained directly in front of him, my back against the wall.

"Hey, Pacifico." Another classmate, Rodney, joined us. "Have you heard that new song by Herman's Hermits?"

"Which one?"

"It's called, 'Mrs. Brown, You've Got a Lovely Daughter.'"

"I don't think so," I answered, my tone restrained.

I moved closer to the wall, and as they talked, I made sure to face them.

The bell clanged, drowning out all voices. At last, recess was over. I returned to my classroom, relieved.

Walking home, I avoided stepping on sidewalk cracks. Someone told me it's bad luck to step on the cracks, so I needed all the help I could get.

I resolved to ask Dad to remove the hardened, caked-on blood from my hair. I couldn't continue to hide the back of my head from everyone each day. *What could I say to Dad?* I feared asking him about anything because he'd get mad. There's no telling what he'd think, do, or say when he found out I went to school with blood on my head.

The right opportunity would have to come up before I could talk to him. On the way home, I rehearsed lines in my head.

It was hard to believe I wanted to ask him for a haircut. His standing over me with scissors always made me nervous. His anger could activate in a split second.

I recalled another time when he had cut my hair. I hadn't slept well and I spent that Saturday morning in the backyard pushing a shovel into unforgiving soil. He held a comb to my scalp and snipped strands of my hair.

The usual fear wasn't enough to keep me upright. The first few times, I caught myself nodding off before my chin slumped to my chest. Finally, weariness overtook me. It was too difficult to sit still with my head straight up like he always demanded.

He had stood behind me in silence. I didn't see it coming. The blow to the side of my head almost knocked me off the chair. He caught me falling asleep. Now a bobbing ocean buoy, I fought to remain erect as a hurricane gust swept over me. "Keep your head up!" he screamed. It took everything to remain conscious. Small bubbles popped in my blurred sight as I struggled to regain my vision.

Haircut

I walked into the usually quiet house. I didn't see him anywhere, though his car sat in the driveway. He didn't have a job. We received welfare and he claimed he was disabled. The joke among my brothers was that Dad didn't seem disabled when he smacked our butts.

He was always home, somewhere. I went to my bedroom and spied him through the blinds, tending to the backyard garden. I changed out of my school clothes and walked to the back.

As I approached, he looked at me without emotion and waited until I stood before him. He directed me to follow behind him to hold the garden hose while he watered the plants. I kept the hose free from obstructions so he could move from plant to plant without restriction. Any snag on my end invited a menacing glare.

"Okay," he said, "turn off the water."

So far, I didn't do anything wrong. I trailed behind him into the kitchen to prepare the evening meal.

He clutched carrots in both hands and brought them to the kitchen counter. When he set them down, I murmured, "Dad, can you cut my hair?"

His eyes looked at me with surprise. I turned and lifted my hair to expose the hardened blood.

"Oh."

I'd never heard him say that simple two-letter word at low volume. I guess he didn't need to be reminded how the wound got there.

I wondered if it angered him that I'd gone to school with blood in my hair. But he said nothing.

When he finished, he uttered a simple "Okay." I hopped off the high chair and returned to the kitchen to cut vegetables.

11

Boiling Over

―――――――――――――――――

"**P**acifico. Pacifico! It's time to wake up." I heard a woman's faint voice. I was heavily sedated in a dentist's chair after eight teeth were extracted.

Most were upper teeth. I was in fourth grade.

I hadn't taught myself to brush my teeth the way I did with tying my shoes. I needed to teach myself to tie my shoes. I tied them differently than others tied theirs, but my way of doing it worked for me.

No one told me the importance of brushing, so I never did. What kid is going to brush his teeth if no one orders him to?

"It's time to go home now." The kind dental assistant nudged my side.

My body felt heavy, and I struggled to wake up.

Finally, my eyes cleared to see the assistant, and Mom standing behind her. Mom regarded me with a blank expression and remained silent.

Not saying a word, I got in the car and Mom drove away. Her eyes remained fixed ahead.

I sat horrified as my tongue tasted blood and probed gaping chasms in my gums. I looked at Mom and wanted comfort. *What happened to me? I'm scared. Why aren't you saying anything?*

She didn't return my gaze and said nothing the whole ride home.

At home, Mom was always there—just not for me. I don't recall her touching me except for a few times. One time when I was a baby, I remember her carrying me in her arms. A couple of times, when I had the flu, she placed the back of her hand to my forehead to gauge my fever. Quickly she withdrew her hand and then gave me aspirin and water. The brief feel of the warmth of her hand had me yearning for more contact.

Dad was thirty-six years old when he married Mom and brought her to the United States from the Philippines.

Mom was only sixteen years old.

Dad dominated her the way he did the rest of us. She was hardly different from other kids in the family. Dad gave orders and everyone—including Mom—followed them. She was emotionally unavailable, even incapable of providing love or affection.

My sisters probably wished Mom could've provided more guidance in the kitchen too.

The pot of rice quivered on the stove. White, boiling liquid lifted the lid up and down, clicking the rim as steam escaped.

"Don't burn the rice!" Dad barked the same all-too-familiar command to family members tasked with rice-cooking duties.

My oldest sister, Cookie, ran to the stove to lower the burner. The boiling stifled, but the pungent odor of burned rice remained.

"I'll be dammed," our father growled, stomping to the pot to assess the damage.

I considered myself lucky I was too young to cook. Preventing rice from burning always seemed precarious. Unless the burner is lowered at precisely the right time, the rice burns. Stopping it from boiling over was like asking leaves not to rustle in the breeze.

Dad scooped rice from the pot into a bowl. When he got to the bottom, he clicked his tongue in disgust and shook his head in disbelief. It angered him when a layer of burned rice stuck to the bottom of the pot because removing the rice required soaking it overnight.

He glowered at Cookie.

Cookie stood to the side, her doe eyes caught in the crosshairs of a hunter's scope. She had nowhere to hide.

Dad shoved the offending pot into the sink, and the pot impacting against porcelain resounded like a head-on collision.

My sister's mouth pursed. Tears streamed from her eyes as she fought to keep from crying aloud.

"If you don't like that, you can get the hell out of here when you're eighteen!" Dad shouted the familiar saying he directed at my older siblings.

At first, I didn't grasp why he wanted them to wait until eighteen. In time, I understood that by law they had to remain until adulthood.

When he yelled those words, I promised myself to do everything perfect so he'd never scream the same thing at me.

12

A Grave Predicament

When Dad stirred a teaspoonful of sugar into his cup of Maxwell House instant coffee, it resounded rhythmically, slowly, and ominously. The sound of his spoon was a weekend message.

It was 6:30 a.m. This meant that at precisely 7:00 a.m. on Saturday and Sunday mornings, Dad would barge into our room to rouse me and my brothers for morning chores.

For the next thirty minutes, my slumber remained fitful while anticipating his arrival.

"Rise and shine!" he pronounced as he yanked the cord of our venetian blinds up and down until he was satisfied we were awake. The aluminum blades clattered and clapped for a rude awakening. I cursed the Venetians for their creation.

After absentminded bites of toast and jam and a small glass of milk, I trailed my brothers to the backyard at 7:30. On a cool Bay Area morning, we stood with hands in pockets awaiting orders.

"Hold this right there," Dad barked. My fingers held one end of the measuring tape to the ground at different locations as he formed a rectangle.

My brothers observed in guarded silence, ready to jump when Dad said how high.

He hammered thin wooden stakes at each corner and tied twine to each stake, marking a four-sided boundary.

"Grab a shovel and dig," he commanded. His glare had me wondering why we hadn't already had shovels in our hands. "Stay inside the rope. Dig two feet deep."

I wondered what kinds of plants we were cultivating. The measurements seemed shorter, wider, and deeper than our usual garden beds.

We dug in silence for some time.

Our father left us alone, but occasionally returned to make sure we remained on task.

When he came back, we had finished to Dad's specifications. The pre-afternoon sun had yet to dispel the morning cool, and we stood knee-deep in the large trench.

"Dig it one foot deeper," he directed. I imagined a grave large enough for the three of us.

We finished excavation as the midday sun beamed overhead. I sat on the side with my legs dangling as if contemplating a jump into a swimming pool. Buster and Scoop stood with shovel handles propped in hand and blades in the ground, surveying the chasm and mounds of earth along the sides.

I anticipated Dad's next order would be to get the wheelbarrow and bring sacks of steer manure to the hole.

"Get all of the comic books in your room and bring them here." I was confused by what we were doing.

We grabbed stacks of comic books from under our beds, inside the closet, and on top of a built-in shelf that ran the length of one wall. My arms extended downward to hold them in both hands.

Dad pointed to the hole and said, "Put them in here."

My heart felt as if a fist closed around it. Sadness and grief gripped me, but I stayed to the task as ordered.

After several trips, the rectangular hole became more than half filled with our comics. The glossy shine of the comic book covers within the gray, earthen hole resembled a patchwork quilt of good versus evil.

I kneeled at the graveside and pondered the final outcome of our collection. A copy of *Thunder Agents* rested in my hands. It wasn't as popular as some of the titles like *Superman* or *Iron Man*, but it was one of my favorites. Others such as *The Uncanny X-Men* caught my attention. Many of these titles were my only solace and escape.

Dad would soon be back after a thorough search of our bedroom.

Grabbing some of my favorites, I hurriedly hid them under boxes and behind the wheelbarrow. Buster and Scoop looked on, amused. I wished for Flash's super speed to gather more.

With only minutes to act, I failed to save many of them. Those fictional heroes had saved me through nightly relief from a troubled life. But in the end, I couldn't save them.

When Dad returned, he uttered what I had dreaded to hear: "Fill the hole."

I gulped and took a final look before hurling my first shovelful. The dirt landed on a fresh copy of *Action Comics*. The flying Superman couldn't escape this earth's gravity. The landing dirt chunks resembled blood spatter from an Alfred Hitchcock movie.

The hole filled, but the grave remained unmarked.

When Dad retired to his room for the evening, I retrieved the few rescued comics from the backyard and hid them under my mattress. Once all the household lights were out, I rested a flashlight on my chest, and my bedsheets formed a cocoon.

At the neighborhood drug store, the chrome comic book tree carousel squeaked during my monthly visits. New tales of my heroes' adventures remained safe under my mattress.

13

Consolation

Friday afternoon at school, I took deliberate steps in front of the class.

"Consolation. David took consolation in seeing what good came out of a bad situation. Consolation."

They put their pencils to paper as I watched. Some students seemed to pause to think about letter order. A few mouthed the word to sound it out, while others shook their heads and appeared to guess. I waited for all but one or two to finish before proceeding to the next word.

On Fridays after lunch, I conducted our makeup spelling test. I rarely had to take it because on Thursday's test, I usually received 100 percent scores. My sixth-grade teacher, Mr. Johnson, allowed me to administer the makeup exam so I wouldn't have to sit and wait for the class to finish.

Through grade school, I usually had the correct answers when my teachers asked me questions. At home, I was motivated to know the answers because I got scolded or physically punished if I didn't.

When I didn't know the answers at school, I felt ashamed, as if I had failed or had done something wrong.

In Mr. Johnson's class, I resolved not to just sit back and take in information, but to ask my own questions.

I observed how some students raised their hands. Others blurted out questions without bothering to raise a hand.

Mr. Johnson had certain pauses in his speech that allowed others to interject.

It took several weeks to drum up the courage to raise my hand.

Mr. Johnson stood in front. "If, for any reason, the president is unable to complete his term, the vice president would then assume his duties." His pressed, white, short-sleeved shirt and tie accentuated his lesson delivery. He paused.

My arm seemed stuck in its socket. I pushed against an unseen barrier. Embarrassment, shame, and fear conspired against me. I reminded myself I was not at home. At worst, I could sprint out the door at the first sign of danger. I urged my hand upward, but only made it halfway.

Mr. Johnson viewed me as if my daily behavior was to naturally ask questions.

"Yes, Pacifico."

"If the vice president were unable to serve, what would happen next?" I looked down at my desk and studied the lead pencil marks streaked on its surface. My face flushed and I felt heated as if I had the flu. I upturned my head to gauge my teacher's contempt.

"In that case, the speaker of the house . . ." His explanation trailed away from my attention. He didn't berate me, nor did he say anything to make me feel stupid. A few students glanced in my direction, but nothing more.

I did it. I'd survived and proved to myself that I deserved to be heard.

In school, I was happy because I performed well in the classroom and on the playground. After returning to my demoralized home existence, I looked forward to bedtime so I could enter the safe world of comic books that eased my mind and gave me hope that the world was good. I regularly bought new titles from the drug store and hid them under my mattress.

Comic books also increased my vocabulary. They enhanced my creativity and imagination. And when conducting spelling tests, I realized I wouldn't have spelled so well if not for the thousands of comic book pages I had read.

One evening, I pulled out three new comic books I had placed under my pillow before leaving for school. They were ripped in half. Dad turned the tables on me. Unlike my heroes, I was powerless and unable to right a wrong.

Underneath my mattress, my small collection lay in pieces. I fell back on my bed, feeling torn in half.

One day when I came home from school, our new dog from the pound strained at his leash, excited to see me. Ebony was small with black, wavy hair. I petted his head and face. He joyously licked my hand.

I came to love Ebony. I thought of him as my dog because he was always excited to see me. He ran to me when I called his name. He arrived hopping from hind feet to forefeet, tail wagging and tongue hanging.

When I entered our house, there was always a pervasive strained, uncertain, and unfriendly environment. No one said anything to me. I received an occasional muted glance from a sibling. At least my dog liked me.

By the end of the year, Cookie turned eighteen and enlisted in the United States Navy. The family exodus had begun.

14

Junior High

Crowds of strangers were threatening to me, so I slowed down as I drew nearer to my junior high school. As I approached the school grounds, I studied the students' movements. After a summer apart, some gathered in groups while others shouted to each other.

I searched for familiar classmates from elementary school. I recognized some, but I didn't know what to say to them. The guys looked bigger than I, and I tensed with apprehension. The girls looked different too. They wore dresses, made up their hair, and had put on makeup.

The last time I had arrived at a new school, I cried without reservation. I didn't do that anymore, but I entered my homeroom uncomfortable and uncertain, and early enough to sit in the back row.

In the weeks to come, elementary school friends found other friendships. Cliques formed, but I never clicked with them. During recess, I walked around by myself.

Lunch hours left me vulnerable and friendless. I pretended to walk purposefully as if I had somewhere to go and didn't have time for others. My usual goal was to find a secluded bench where I could sit alone.

I didn't belong or fit in anywhere.

On a section of our living room wall, our school report cards were posted like fugitives' photos at the post office. Thumbtacks pressed them to the wall for family viewing. Tack holes from past quarters dotted the wall, resembling smallpox on an adolescent face. Grades of less than an A were circled with a bright red felt pen.

Penny and Scoop were the academic stars. Penny rarely received less than an A grade. Dad kept on her for it. He devised Spanish-lesson flashcards and drilled her relentlessly. "What's wrong with you?" was Dad's usual refrain when she couldn't come up with the word or pronounced it incorrectly. In addition to his native Filipino language, Dad spoke fluent Spanish. His expectation was for her to be flawless.

Scoop got Dad's attention when a rare B showed imperfection. "History?" Dad said, "You can't read a history book? Isn't that something?"

After experiencing academic success in elementary school, I attended junior high certain I didn't want the same expectations he had of Penny or Scoop thrust on me. At home, and also at school, I hoped to remain below Dad's radar. I strategized to receive Cs and Bs, with an occasional A. Red circles on my report cards meant success to me. I wouldn't receive the same scrutiny as I would if I obtained straight As.

My grade reports gave Dad opportunities to declare, "You'll never amount to anything." I stood a foot in front of him while he studied my face, perhaps expecting me to nod in agreement. "You can't do it!" His voice rose as if he were an attorney making closing arguments. I maintained a blank look, knowing any reaction prompted further scorn or physical attack.

In time, Dad's educational expectations of me lowered, and he left me alone.

The door leading from the garage into the kitchen flew open, and the crash of the door against the wall petrified me. The door didn't become unhinged, but Dad sure did. I cleared the breakfast table, hoping I wasn't the one he hunted. He stomped past me, and I breathed in relief. He stalked toward my oldest brother, Pat, asleep in his room after a late-night shift at the local chicken eatery. It was a quiet Saturday morning until then.

"Get up!" Dad roared. He kicked the bed. "I told you not to park over the line!" The line referred to a foot-wide section of concrete laid down a month earlier to widen the driveway.

When I peered through the garage at my brother's navy blue AMC Rambler, I saw that the right front tire rested inches over the edge of the new concrete.

"Move your damn car!" Dad howled in full rage.

Pat, with a look of fatigue and stunned disbelief on his face, trudged to the garage.

"If you don't like that, you can get out!" Dad blistered at him from behind.

Pat had recently turned eighteen. Two weeks after this incident, he left home.

In view of the second family departure, I vowed to be the one to earn Dad's approval. I would do as I was told and not say anything to raise his ire. I didn't want to experience the painful rejection of his screaming at me to leave by the time I turned eighteen.

Dad wiped down the stovetop while I hung laundry on our indoor clothesline. Penny washed pots and pans in the kitchen sink. Cleaning the stainless-steel, copper-bottomed pots was difficult, especially after cooking rice. Dad threw tantrums if the copper bottoms were not in perfect, spotless condition.

"I told you!" Dad erupted as he grabbed a pot from the drain rack. "These are not done right!"

I heard a dull thump, like testing the ripeness of a watermelon. I guessed he hit her with the pot or threw it at her. In a violent clatter, the pot came to rest under the kitchen table.

As Dad withdrew, he had spittle on one side of his mouth—like a rabid dog.

Penny remained at the sink, whimpering and defeated. Her arms and hands dangled within the plastic washbasin like untied shoestrings. Tears streamed from her eyes, falling into the lukewarm soapy water.

Not long after, Penny accepted a scholarship to attend the University of California, Berkeley. Toward the end of summer, she moved.

15

Spoiled Sports

F ew things deliver more joy to young boys than to play tackle football in the mud. Morning rains gave way to an afternoon of clear blue skies with cotton-candy clouds. The rectangular expanse of turf facing the street in front of the high school's administrative offices offered the perfect setting for our football game. There were no adults, no coaches, and no referees—just us boys in jeans and T-shirts romping over wet grass.

On the first play, I spied one of the neighborhood kids, Lloyd, scampering in the open, carrying the ball in hopes of a clear path to the end zone. With a running start, I threw my body at full speed onto his. The impact kicked up splashes of muddy water and clods of grass, leaving a furrowed path.

Lloyd pulled himself up to see who had upset his run. A broad grin and elated eyes greeted me. "We skidded about ten feet!"

"That was like a Slip 'N Slide." I laughed with him.

I turned my head toward the T-intersection at the back entrance to Safeway and saw Mom's car sitting at the stop sign. The car didn't move. With the sun's reflection on the windshield, I couldn't tell if she was in the car, but after several double takes, I made out the silhouette of her long hair. I returned to the huddle, happy with the thought that my mother wanted to see her son at play.

For the next play, I lined up on the left side, closest to the street, to permit a better view for Mom.

"Hut one, hut two . . . hike!" Albert barked.

I streaked down the side. By midfield, my defender trailed by five yards. Albert lofted the ball my way. The football rose in an arc, and as it descended, I concentrated on the ball's spiral, slowing my run so as not to break stride. It arrived in my hands, where I cradled it against my side and broke for the touchdown.

"Yay!" my teammates yelled, clapping their hands. I grinned, waved back, and retraced my steps toward the huddle.

At the intersection, Mom still sat in her car. Slowly, her car veered to the right and headed home.

That one's for Mom. The thought warmed me, certain she was proud to see her youngest son score a touchdown.

Pride lifted me on my walk home because my mother had seen me play. I wondered what her reaction would be, although she rarely talked to me. In the past, she never mentioned my outstanding report cards. Even when I presented grade school Mother's Day projects to her, she didn't express thanks or even ask what I created. This time she'd at least flash me a smile.

When I entered the house, Mom stood at the kitchen table cutting vegetables. I peered at her with a cautious smirk pasted on my face. She returned my glance, but her expression was filled with irritation. "Don't play there again," she muttered.

What? It was like a blindside tackle that sent me careening out of bounds. Crushed, I continued to my room, not bothering to ask why. Was it because my clothes were wet and muddy? Or were school grounds closed on weekends?

Mom hadn't cared if I had fun or scored a touchdown.

In later years, I rationalized and consoled myself that perhaps she may have wanted to protect me if Dad found out. But I'll never know.

After a day of school and completed household chores, I rested on the sofa. Scoop sat at the other end. The late afternoon sun projected rays of light onto the coffee table.

On the table lay an unfolded copy of the *Milpitas Post*, our local community newspaper, with a front-page photo of Scoop swinging at a tennis ball. The headline read: "Super Soph." I picked up the paper. It described his sophomore season, naming him one of the top players in the Central Coast Section. He had finished with a 14–2 record. The newspaper also named him as the probable starting point guard for the basketball team in the fall. Wow!

A knock on the door startled me. Dad opened it.

"Hi, Frank." Our neighbor across the street, Mr. Paulin, greeted Dad. Dad motioned him inside, but Mr. Paulin stayed one step inside the door frame.

"I just saw in the paper about your son playing on the tennis team. That's very impressive." He glanced at Scoop, then me, and returned to Dad. "I just wanted to congratulate you." Years before, Mr. Paulin's son had garnered acclaim as a shot-putter. It was kind of him to recognize my brother's accomplishments.

"Yeah, yeah. That's good," Dad replied in a subdued tone. "Thanks for coming by." Dad shook his hand and calmly shut the door.

He listened to Mr. Paulin's footsteps fade down the walkway.

Then he turned and zeroed in on Scoop. "You're no good. That's nothing!"

Scoop remained still.

"Two losses! What's that?" Dad pressed. "You can't do it. You're too small."

Fourteen varsity wins and only two losses! That was amazing! I didn't see what height had to do with anything either.

At that point, I decided not to play high school tennis, although my older siblings had. And despite my love of sinking long-range jumpers on the playground, neither would I try out for the basketball team.

My school playing days were over before they started.

16

The Last Link

I headed home after school to report for household duties. The half-mile walk between Ayer High School and home wouldn't take long. On a bright, sunny, late afternoon, I wondered what chores awaited me.

Mom worked swing shift as an electronics assembler at Fairchild Camera and Instrument in Mountain View. As I strolled home, she again drove right by me on her way to work, never looking or waving at me. She couldn't have missed me. I was walking up the street she was driving down. There was plenty of time and distance to see me. Was she really that cold? Had she hidden herself in a life of total numbness?

In my neighborhood, I heard what sounded like a radio station frequency coming in and out.

When I neared my house, I realized the sounds were not from a radio but Dad yelling so loud that I heard him from down the street. *But at whom?*

I presumed some poor door-to-door salesman had discovered what *no* meant to Dad.

An unyielding racket came through the front door. I couldn't make out words, but I slowly opened the entryway and discovered the target of Dad's tirade—Scoop. The rant concerned his playing on the basketball team.

Now a high school junior, Scoop defied and argued with Dad when he could. They were like the same guy—prideful, arrogant, and angry.

I didn't think anyone in the family could win with Dad as long as we lived at home. Too many times, the backtalk from my older brothers and sisters led to Dad holding grudges and pressing harder on them weeks and months later.

"I'm on the team. I'm going. I have to play," Scoop interjected between Dad's verbal blasts.

"You're a son of a bitch!"

"Yeah, and you're my father." Scoop said it loud enough for only me to hear.

Good one. I was usually the one who played on words. I looked downward and pursed my lips. If Dad noticed my smirk, I would be the next focus of his onslaught.

As I put away my things in my bedroom, I saw Scoop scale the back fence. I guessed he didn't want Dad to see him exit the front door.

A basket of washed laundry awaited me when I walked out to the front room. Dad nodded toward the basket. "I guess he left you holding the bag."

I hung damp garments on hangers and hoisted them to the nailed beams above the hallway heater.

"You're the *last link*," Dad said, his voice filled with resignation.

What does that mean? A link is a circular piece on a chain. The last link holds keys. I remained befuddled. Whatever it was, I didn't want to be it.

"Yes, you're the *last link*," he repeated.

In the months and years to come, he reiterated this declaration. Although he never explained its meaning, and I never asked, to me it meant he considered me the *last link* of my siblings to appease him. Despite their academic and athletic accomplishments, none met his satisfaction.

The theme to *Mission: Impossible* played in my head, followed by the opening dialogue: "Your mission, should you decide to accept it, is to gain your dad's approval where others before you have failed. This tape will self-destruct in five seconds. Good luck, Peewee."

The recording never dissolved like it did on the TV show. It played repeatedly for the remainder of my time at home as I continued to hang laundry, paint the house, dig holes in the garden, prepare dinner, and not disrespect him.

The Last Link

My mission was to be what the others were not—compliant.

My first year in high school established me again on the periphery,— the same as in junior high—unable, or not knowing how, to be involved. I had few friends at school. The ones whom I played pickup games with on the playground drifted away to join school teammates.

Throughout high school, many of my friends were dropouts or attended continuation high school. When I visited their homes, I saw that they lived in dysfunctional and abusive situations similar to mine. One had a drunken father who was a sailor and swore like one. Another lived in a home where it seemed they didn't own a vacuum cleaner. On occasion, I observed children fending for themselves at dinnertime, eating only baloney sandwiches.

Occasionally, I met with friends who didn't go to school. After I cut classes, I'd share a cigarette with them at the local 7-Eleven. They didn't have any plans beyond someday moving out and getting a job.

I wanted to go to continuation school where some of these friends went. However, I maintained a C average. That passing grade kept me out. Otherwise, I wouldn't have heard the end of it from Dad.

At Ayer High School, I didn't belong to any group, except maybe the stoners who were known for partying. I had long hair and wore a Levi jacket.

For the most part, I didn't belong anywhere.

During my freshman year, Buster continued the family exodus and enlisted in the US Army after he turned eighteen.

Three Cruz kids remained at home: Scoop, Mimi, and me.

Dad left Mimi alone, excused from any responsibilities. She was six years younger than me. We supported each other, spending many evenings listening to AM radio, playing who could be first to yell out the song title or artist of each song.

Scoop was allowed to keep his academic and sports commitments.

As when I was a child, the household chores fell to me, the last link.

17

Name Shame

***

I was thrilled to cruise with Dickey in his Ford Maverick, which was decorated with white racing stripes that curved over the hood and trunk. Massive, wide rear tires gave his ride a drag-racing, funny-car look, attracting frozen-in-place stares.

Dickey was a senior. His best friend, Kenny, rode shotgun. I sat in back with two sophomore buddies.

"You dudes wanna go to the youth center?" Dickey said, turning his head to us in back. "They got pool tables there."

I'd never been to a youth center. I didn't know what one was, but I liked to shoot pool. "Cool," I replied.

We pulled into the Milpitas Youth Center parking lot, and the five of us piled out. The glass entrance door resembled Safeway's. Dickey pushed through and led us inside.

A tall, lean guy with combed-back, slick black hair greeted us. Fluorescent overhead lighting reflected off the lenses of his black-framed glasses.

"Hi, guys! Welcome to the Milpitas Youth Center. My name's Ricardo. What're your names?"

"Dickey."

"Kenny."

As we filed in, Ricardo extended a bro-handshake to each of us.

"Mike."

I brought up the rear. Unease clogged my breathing in anticipation of my introduction. I had two choices for a name. Pacifico seemed reserved for teachers and doctors. Each year on the first day of school, I had to remind myself during roll call, *I'm Pacifico.* I didn't attach to Pacifico because family and friends called me Peewee.

I detested Peewee, and always had, especially since I had grown into a teenager. Peewee made me feel small, less than unworthy. It symbolized a troubled life inside and outside of my house. I may as well have been named Puny.

"Russell."

"Thanks for coming, Russell."

My turn. I extended an apprehensive handshake.

In a lame attempt to avoid humiliation, I went with "Pacifico."

Ricardo clasped my hand, but his grip loosened. "What? Say that again?"

"Pacifico."

His eyes narrowed as if he were reading small print.

"Pasisisko? Pasisco? Pacheco? Where'd you get that?"

"My parents named me that." There was no averting this calamity. Thank goodness I didn't tell him I go by Peewee.

"Well, come in, whatever your name is." He shook his head, still at a loss.

A few of my friends looked back, curious. My face must've reddened into the color of a cactus pear.

Each ball on the pool table clicked sharply in the same way my thoughts smacked against each other, stricken by the shame of my names.

In the eight years since moving to Milpitas, I remained curious about what had become of our old, crumbling house. Was it still standing? Were the orchards still there?

One Saturday after morning chores, I satisfied my curiosity.

I rode my green hand-me-down Schwinn ten speed to San Jose.

It was a warmer fall day than normal. As I rode farther into San Jose, doubt crept into my mind. *Turn around now. What if you can't find the house? What if you make a wrong turn? What if you get too tired to come back?*

What if you get a flat tire? I lowered my head and clutched the handlebars, determined to reach my destination.

The hot weather pressed around me. Waves of heat wiggled off the pavement. I had bicycled five miles and was weary.

I turned toward my old home. The area hadn't changed much since we'd left. I pedaled slowly. A row of small houses along the lower section of the long road reconnected me to younger days.

A hump in the road sectioned off an area near to neighbors, most of whom we never knew. They lived in large, modern houses, with big windows and wide curving driveways. I don't think we knew them because it was too far to walk. Plus, we were just poor farm workers.

A final marker would tell me I was near. Adjacent to one of the houses, a lone, towering peach tree still flourished. My mouth watered at recollections of chomping its juicy, plump fruits.

I slowed and looked toward the house—that wasn't there.

Pedaling farther, I rolled to a stop. Only a clearing remained. When we had lived there, the house was almost uninhabitable, so I wasn't surprised it was gone. Still, I had hoped to at least see a boarded-up house.

I slumped on top of my bike, reminiscing about my childhood home, thankful that the shade of fruit trees provided shelter from the sun.

After a while, I considered the long ride back to Milpitas.

"You used to live there, didn't you?" A soft, even voice broke my contemplation.

Across the narrow road, with a backdrop of apricot trees, a young Asian girl, not much older than I, straddled her bicycle. She observed me, waiting for my answer.

"Yeah." I said nothing more, confused by her sudden appearance. I didn't recognize her.

"What's your name?"

"Peewee. That's what they called me when I lived here."

"That's your name . . ." She paused before her next statement. "But I feel that I want to call you Pete."

Her comment rushed over me like grain unloading from a silo. I turned to the vacant lot, where my house once stood.

"Why?" I spun back and asked.

She was gone.

I twisted to look behind me. She wasn't biking down the road.

I stooped to handlebar level to peer underneath the orchard canopy. Not there either.

Like a frantic owl, I swiveled my head, surveying the landscape, searching for a girl on a bicycle. Again, nothing.

Where had she gone? I had turned for only a second. Why did she leave without saying anything?

Squeezing the handlebars, I pushed myself upright in an effort to get a grip on reality. It felt surreal and unreal. Maybe the hot weather and fatigue from the ride got to me. Maybe I imagined the whole thing.

I couldn't have. And I didn't.

Was Rod Serling of *The Twilight Zone* standing somewhere in front of a cherry tree? "Imagine, if you will, a lone bicycle rider . . ."

During the trip home, my conversation with the young girl replayed in my mind. She said she wanted to call me Pete. *Why? What does that mean?*

In the weeks to come, thoughts concerning my name as *Pete* collided like bumper cars. *Pete. Pete Cruz.* I envisioned reaching out a confident handshake. *Hello, my name is Pete.* I liked it.

As a teenager, I was a passionate basketball fan and idolized Pete Maravich. He was inducted into the NBA Hall of Fame at the end of his career and was later named one of the top seventy-five players of all time. He threw rare behind-the-back and no-look passes. In a league of fundamentals, Pete was flamboyance and creativity, a Beatles-like basketball player with long hair and floppy socks.

Pete Maravich cemented my desire to change my name to Pete.

18

Name Change

"**P**ass me that doobie! Don't bogart it." Russell used slang terms for a marijuana cigarette and for holding it too long. After dinnertime, down the street from me, we huddled inside Chuck's garage. The single light bulb on the wall cast a subdued glow.

"Bite me, man. Here." Chuck passed the joint to him.

Russell took a strong drag. The lit end flared like a brake light. The hiss of the toke gave way to a lengthy curl of smoke.

How would my friends take my request to call me by another name? Most of us grew up blocks from each other, so Peewee was a given. Still, anxiety skated in my stomach and kicked up icy slivers. I hoped the marijuana high made them agreeable.

"This is good stuff," Dirk said, as he passed me the joint.

"Guys, I have something to tell you." I eyed each of them. Normally, I injected humorous observations or friendly putdowns into our get-togethers. My grim manner must have seized their attention. They stopped talking and looked at me.

"Serious?" Russell said.

"Yeah, I guess so."

"Okay, man. Go ahead. I'm listening," Mike said. I'd known him since the third grade when his family moved to Jupiter Drive.

"I don't want to be called Peewee anymore. Or Pacifico. Some of you don't even know that's my real name."

"Keep that joint going. Pass it on," Chuck said, reminding us of our original priority. The others faced me with noncommittal but curious expressions.

"What would you want us to call you?" Robert said.

"Pete."

"Pete?" Dirk nodded. "Okay, cool."

Russell added, "Yeah, if you don't like your name and want to be called something different, that's up to you."

"I know it won't change just like that. I might have to remind you once in a while."

"Hey, no problem, bro," Mike said. "Pete."

We filed out to the backyard to finish building our fort. At the rear corner of the backyard, the back fence and neighbor's fence served as walls. Large plywood sheets composed the other two walls and the roof. Our fort fit at least ten people.

The fort functioned mainly as our smoking room. Our gatherings were supposed to be private, but one time, a passerby on the other side of the fence warned us concerning the large volume of smoke seeping through the slats.

A few days later, we sat in the fort. Inside was black as midnight, except for a few narrow shafts of light slicing through the gaps. We couldn't see each other's faces.

The red bead of the reefer passed from hand to hand like a honeybee floating from flower to flower.

Scraping noise from the plywood door being pulled across the ground shook us from our cannabis-induced haze. Smoke wafted up and outward as we turned our heads away to shield our eyes from the intruding rays of the sun.

Dickey crowded in, and we shuffled our seats to make room.

"Hey, dudes. Pass that joint over here," he said. "Who's here? Is Pete here?"

His question startled me. It was the first feedback since my name-change announcement.

"Yeah, I'm right here."

"Cool. What's happening, man?"

Dickey and I weren't close friends because he was a senior.

By asking for "Pete," Dickey issued his stamp of approval. Anyone having a problem with my changing from Peewee would now answer to him. My heart warmed with gratitude.

Later, I realized Dickey probably related to my anguish. For a while, he wanted to be called *Dick*. We didn't dare tease him. He eventually settled on *Richard*.

I sat on top of the cold, unforgiving concrete at Chuck's front door, waiting for his return.

It had rained during the day, and drizzly conditions dampened my face, jacket, and mood. Occasional raindrops made widening circles on a brownish puddle on the worn lawn.

Chuck bounded up the walkway. His appearance jolted me from my cold huddle.

"Hey, Peewee. Pete."

"Hey, Chuck."

"Peewee, Pete, Peewee." He laughed while standing over me. "What a name!"

In the big-dog hierarchy among teenage boys, I never considered myself smaller than anyone.

"Hey, little Peewee."

I got off the ground. Was he high? Had he been drinking? If so, I held an advantage over his impairment. He outweighed me by maybe thirty pounds, but to me, bigness equated to slowness.

"Peewee, how funny," he continued. His pupils enlarged in delight. I also remembered he smoked cigarettes at a pack a day. He couldn't last against me. "Hey, little Peewee." He laughed again. My final advantage: an overflowing reservoir of anger when it came to my name.

"Take it back or I'll take you down." I glared at his face, smoldering.

"Little Peewee, what you gonna do?"

I pulled him downward and squeezed him in a headlock, enlisting my body weight to weaken his neck. From countless bouts with my older brothers, I knew leverage. His leg bent forward and I ushered his other leg inward by shoving my foot behind his knee. He resisted, but rage surged through me. He buckled and fell to both knees on the soggy grass.

"Now do you take it back?" I breathed the question into his ear, maintaining the headlock. He said nothing, and I applied my full weight to his neck and head. He bent to all fours and faced the sodden earth.

"I said you're going down unless you take it back."

He gasped for breath.

My fury remained redlined. "What do you say now?"

He remained mute.

I steered him to the mud puddle in the yard and stabilized my two feet on the cement walkway. On the lawn, he had no traction on the slippery grass.

"Your face is going into the water unless you take it back." I held him steady above the pooled mud beneath him, my wrath mushrooming. I pushed his head downward. He offered little resistance to my consuming anger.

His teasing had triggered all the times I'd been made fun of, all the times I'd been ridiculed, all the times I'd been made to feel small.

With his face inches from immersion, his eyes widened in fear. "I take it back. I take it back."

His voice sounded too composed and too unhurried—unrepentant, if anything. I wondered if he gave up just so I'd let him up. I wanted him to know my humiliation. I wanted nothing to do with Peewee again. I held him like a cobra's maw clamped on its victim.

"Not good enough," I said. "Now, say 'Uncle.'"

Silence accompanied the cold and the rain.

Pulling him steadily downward, his nose was an inch from wet payback.

"Uncle," he said.

"One more time."

"Uncle." He finally believed his dunking was going to be reality.

I released my hold and watched him stand up, ready to body slam him should he say Peewee again. "Sorry man, I didn't mean to make fun of you." The delight in his eyes of making fun of me was replaced by defeat.

"Don't ever mention that name again. I don't like it, and you won't either."

He never did. Instead, he told others how I was too quick, too tough.

That night established something I had increasingly suspected. Anger made me strong and fearless. It righted any wrongs. It protected me. It kept people away from me.

From that day forward, all my friends regarded me as Pete.

Johnny Cash's "A Boy Named Sue" had nothing on me.

19

Whipped

Scoop and I walked briskly through the neighborhood streets on our way home. As usual, we didn't converse much. The streets were quiet, except for random retirees in their yards. Most people were at their jobs until five o'clock.

The sun gleamed, and mild temperatures made for a pleasant afternoon.

As we passed one house, the garage was open and unattended. At the entrance, two fishing poles, one red and one gold, lay on the floor, reels attached. I didn't care much for fishing, and I'm not sure Scoop did either. But the temptation to ignore it was too great. I kept walking, but Scoop drifted toward the open garage.

Scoop soon caught up to me with a rod in each hand and satisfaction on his face. I was only glad he didn't get caught.

At home, Scoop stashed the stolen goods under his bed.

I settled into an armchair in the living room. Scoop followed and sat on the sofa. Mom ironed shirts at the ironing board. With the house so quiet, I wondered what would happen if I switched on the TV. I never asked if I could turn it on because I was usually rebuffed at the mere suggestion.

"Where'd you get these?" Dad materialized in front of Scoop, clutching the two fishing poles.

Dad must've seen Scoop walk in with the gear.

Scoop sat stunned.

"Where did you get these?" Menace punctuated Dad's words. Scoop's eyes widened, unable to reply, knowing any answer would be the wrong answer.

Dad set the objects on the coffee table. He raced away and returned, gripping the thin belt. "Get up," he commanded.

Scoop rose upright.

"I ask you one more time. Where did you get these?" Dad fingered the belt buckle like the trigger of a gun.

Say your friend gave them to you, say you bought them or found them in a garbage can; say something—anything. I kept quiet, too afraid Dad might turn to me for answers.

Scoop remained silent.

Dad swung his arm as if throwing a fastball to home plate. The leather produced a wicked snap against Scoop's flesh. Dad went into a whipping frenzy, striking him repeatedly and relentlessly. Scoop held his arms out front, but failed to fend off most of the stinging blows.

"Where?" Dad interjected several times.

Scoop turned and twisted, absorbing the all-angled bites of a viper. He gasped and emitted singular "Oh's" and "Ow's." Then he collapsed to the ground, writhing in pain.

Dad continued to attack. His eyes were trancelike, devoid of feeling. He was on a sole mission to inflict suffering.

I stared, an impotent, helpless witness, hoping Dad's arm would get tired. I felt guilty relief that I wasn't the one who stole the fishing gear.

How many times did Dad swing his arm? Fifty? One-hundred? My stomach clenched, guessing that it was many more.

A berserk maniac, he continued the assault.

Mom observed from the side, in the same dispassionate, detached way she always did. During other times like this, I wondered if she had to suppress her emotions to endure watching her children's abuse. Or had she let her heart die and become totally detached? She never intervened. Today was no different, until she uttered one word.

"Tumigil," Mom said. It came from her lips so softly that I was surprised Dad heard her. I guessed she told him "Stop" or "Enough." Growing up, we never learned Tagalog, the Filipino language. Whatever she said worked.

Dad snapped out of it. He stood over Scoop, the belt drooping like a tendril from a hanging basket. His face reminded me of the times he watched the giant rooster attack me as a little boy.

I followed Scoop to our bedroom.

He didn't cry during the carnage and he didn't now, but his eyes watered. He turned his back to peel off his shirt. With each careful pull upward, he let out a gasp. His back resembled a macabre game of tic-tac-toe etched on flesh. His cross-hatched wounds glistened red, some threatening to drip.

The sheer brutality made this incident different from all others. None of us ever spoke about it again. I let the event descend into my mind's lockbox, afraid it might pop open and spill its ugly contents.

That was the only time I ever saw Mom rescue any of her kids—perhaps she was feeling the pain because she had no one to rescue her.

20

Inflamed

"**Here, take a** look." The head dermatologist motioned to two other clinicians in white coats and pocket protectors.

At the Santa Clara Valley Medical Center, cold drafts from the examination room's air conditioner brushed my exposed arms and legs.

The doctor's faces alternately moved in and about me, like used-car buyers inspecting a vehicle. When one paused or stepped back, the other two maneuvered closer.

There was plenty to see. On different areas of my body, open sores oozed a substance not unlike molasses in texture and color. The largest lesion on the back of my thigh was an angry, gaping eruption that had soaked my pant leg with pus. Other areas had dried to a crusty, golden color.

"Amazing," one doctor said after requesting I move my long hair away from my ear. My ears also seeped. Until then, I had ignored their speculations, but his remark implied I was not normal.

I had expected to receive a prescription for pills and lotion and be cured. Far from it.

My whole body itched and I scratched it. My scratching opened more sores. Some areas crystallized like honey. Once dried, they itched and I scratched them open again, leaving flakes of skin and pus. I could not stop scratching. Nor could I sleep. The immense excretions on the back of my thigh and my right arm stuck to my bedsheets. The doctors diagnosed acute eczema.

They treated it with an array of lotions, which did little to stop my scratching. They even tried a light-spectrum lamp, theorizing certain frequencies would heal me.

To my horror, Dad tried rubbing alcohol. It stung like scalding water. The wounds closed, only to open minutes later.

At school, I remained conscious of my body's intense inflammation. In the spring semester of my sophomore year, during a time when most teenagers worry about acne, mine were like zits on steroids. I grew scales and vigorously scraped them off, only to have them grow back.

Any notions of dating vanished. My skin problems added to my already low self-esteem. I considered myself very athletic, and I took pride in a body I could manage. Now I had no control.

I squirmed in my classroom seats, discreetly wrestling with scratching fits, unable to think of anything to distract myself.

On warm days, I wore long sleeves.

My life was hell. I was a leper.

My favorite class, PE, came to a crushing halt. I cherished the physical and mental release sports competition gave me to cope with life. But I requested enrollment in Adaptive PE for boys who couldn't attend the regular class.

Dressing in gym clothes or being seen in the shower seemed out of the question. I feared my skin would create unwanted attention and I would be shunned.

In Adaptive PE, we sat around doing a lot of nothing. There was a ping-pong table, but no one wanted to play. Some played board games, but I considered them bored games.

I felt helpless. Hopeless.

21

Back in the Game

The asphalt of the middle school playground and overcast skies framed my way of life—gray and desolate. I played basketball there by myself, staying away from the high school grounds and public courts because rarely did anyone happen by there.

During the spring of my junior year, I couldn't bear Adaptive PE anymore. Sometimes we only played checkers. Regular PE had been one of the few places where I escaped my troubles. I experienced sheer joy in competitive play, and I dearly missed it.

While the Adaptive PE class bowled inside the gym using plastic balls and pins, the regular class concluded its basketball unit on the outside blacktop.

Despite the unsightliness of my skin, I longed to rejoin the regular PE class. The timing seemed right, during the chill of the last weeks before springtime. I wore long underwear beneath my gym shorts and PE shirt, hoping my classmates assumed my coverings were due to the cold weather.

For the last day of the basketball unit, Coach Malchow wanted two teams composed of five players to go against each other. He'd select the teams and instruct the rest of the class to observe how all they'd been learning was incorporated into a single game.

"Cruz, take the point." Coach Malchow summoned me as his final pick. I was surprised because it was my first day back in the regular class.

I was in his class as a freshman, so he was familiar with my abilities. My team reversed gym shirts to its gold-colored underside.

A few classmates glanced at me while I switched, perhaps curious about my long underwear.

Coach explained the rules and his expectations for teamwork, defense, and offense. He blew the whistle.

I recognized that in cold weather the ball would be harder to the touch and would be heavier. It'd take more effort to bounce and shoot the ball. I knew that because I had played alone in the cold for so long.

My long johns gave me the unexpected benefit of staying warm and playing loose. The familiar joy of playing with others returned.

Aaron Wills, a senior starting forward on the varsity squad, grinned and shook his head as I sank another long jump shot. All the days of shooting by myself had paid off. My physical appearance or what I wore didn't matter. I was in the zone.

Occasionally, Coach stopped play to make observations, ask questions, or draw up plays. The rest of the time, he kept score and refereed.

"Tie game. Next basket wins," Coach Malchow said.

We went back and forth without scoring.

"Cruz, finish this," he yelled. I suspected he wanted us to dress and shower so he wouldn't get complaints about arriving late to our next classes.

Like pieces on a chessboard, I looked for the defense to move, and I dribbled up the court. I waited at the top of the key for a defender to approach, and then I crossed right to left, zoomed into the open lane, and bounded the ball off the backboard for a layup.

"Gold shirts win," the coach announced.

When I handed the ball to him, I smiled. I expected Coach to say, "Good job." Instead, he frowned and uttered, "You should be doing that on the school team."

Aaron walked into the locker room and stopped when he saw me at a bench. He grinned and shook his head.

"I couldn't throw the ball into the ocean. You were really good." Coming from him, praise poured over me like a warm salve. That year, he had received a scholarship to play at Chico State University.

Maybe if my home circumstances had been different, I could've played for our high school team too. Not being able to join a team left an empty spot in my heart, and my life, that never was filled.

I stalled for others to dress and leave so I could shower.

David Rosen, a short, mousy student sat next to me and made no move to gather his things. He had just finished Adaptive PE.

Peeling my thermals to my knees, I uncovered sores on my thighs and sides of my legs, grateful that the lesions in plain sight had closed. They stuck out like knots on trees.

"What's on your legs?" David said.

"A rash."

"Uh rash." Coach Duke, the teacher for Adaptive PE, walked by mimicking and mocking me. His voice dripped with sarcasm.

The man had a reputation as a world-class jerk. I didn't think anyone liked him, even other coaches. That's why he got stuck teaching Adaptive PE.

"Uh rash," his voice trailed off again. He grinned like a weasel, happy with no one but himself.

After removing the remainder of my gym clothes, I headed to the showers, conscious not only of the external marks on my body, but also of the internal wounding from the coach.

The warm jet spray from the shower soothed me. A few others in the showers glanced at me, but remained unfazed.

I continued wearing my thermals, and when the weather warmed, wore a T-shirt and shorts in PE without incident.

At school, I again found joy and release in PE class. But outside of school, I escaped by getting stoned and drunk.

My skin problems plagued me throughout high school. It was only after graduation that I found help and relief.

22

Dog Gone It!

By the fall of my junior year in high school, Scoop had left home to attend UC Berkeley on a math scholarship. Five of my six siblings gone. Only Mimi and I remained.

Most weekends and some mornings before school, I worked as a baker at Winchell's Donut House. And at home I once again carried the load. Mimi was old enough, but Dad never asked her to do anything. Now Dad was even more demanding of me.

I was his chosen last link.

One day after school, as I entered the garage, my dog was gone. Ebony's corner was empty and swept clean. His leash, his food and water bowls, and his bedding had been removed.

Ebony was always happy to see me when I got home; no one else ever was. He stood on his hind legs, restrained by his tether, wanting me to pat his head.

A sinking blackness crept into my stomach.

Where's my dog? What happened to him?

When I stepped into the kitchen, Dad glared at me. I don't know if he was wondering if I'd say anything. I said nothing; neither did he.

After I went to my room and put my school things away, I changed my clothes and joined him in the garage for daily chores.

Where'd my dog go? Should I ask him? Can I ask him?

What would be the consequences if I were to raise the subject, I wondered. He'd yell at me for questioning him. He'd follow with a physical strike. He'd tell me he left Ebony at the dog pound.

I didn't want to hear the answer. He'd probably rant about my foolishness for caring about a dog.

Without saying a word, I followed the family rule that forbade questioning Dad. Ebony would remain another unspoken subject like the death of my younger brother, Perry.

———

Now that Buster and Scoop were gone, I had my own room, although I wasn't allowed to close my bedroom door. Sometimes Dad used the bathroom at the end of the hallway just to see what I was doing. His own bathroom was closer. He didn't respect my privacy.

When I wasn't roaming the streets, I spent most evenings reading books or listening to Top 40 music in my room. Those two things helped me survive being at home. Dad had backed off his destructive vigilance of my comic books. Still, I remained careful about leaving them in plain sight in case he again decided he no longer liked my reading or collecting them.

My head propped against the wall as I lay on my bed waiting for my favorite rock songs by Creedence Clearwater Revival, Led Zeppelin, or Elton John to play on the radio. Many times, Mimi joined me. We listened to the first stanzas and then blurted out the artist names and song titles.

I took a speaker from a broken radio and connected it to my small bedside clock radio. The uncovered speaker vibrated back and forth within my bookshelf's walls. The hollow bookshelf acted like a speaker box and produced full resonance with deep base.

My ingenuity made me proud. I mouthed the words and strummed my air guitar as I lay on my bed.

"Turn it down!" Dad shouted from the living room. I adjusted the sound to where I could still make out the lyrics.

Dad's figure framed within the doorway. "I told you to turn it down," he growled. With fists clenched, his eyes blazed.

Jerking to an upright position, I worried he'd transform into a rhino and charge. Instead, he seethed. His eyes followed the connecting wire from my radio to the speaker inside the shelf.

"You broke the radio," he said.

My creating something better was to him breaking it.

"You made the radio worse," he added. An object of pride to me was disrespect to him.

As I feared, he charged. But not at me. He seized my radio with both hands, raised it overhead, and hurled the offending device on the floor.

The radio crashed and cracked at its seams.

With tape and wire, I could put it back together. But then he stomped on it. His heavy boot separated the inner workings from its casing.

He stomped again. My radio's inner pieces flew about my bedroom floor.

"Don't ever do that again!" he said, and angrily stalked away.

Collapsing on my bed, I felt shattered like my radio, now an obscene and grotesque sight.

My tears wouldn't flow. I was helpless against his latest onslaught on my psyche. My heart clenched as I picked up the radio's pieces.

My Honda 350 motorcycle waited in the garage, ever a trusted symbol of my loner status. It was a hand-me-down bike from Buster when he left for overseas duty in the service. During times when I felt defenseless at the hands of my father, my motorcycle allowed me release. I straddled it and thrust my leg downward for the kick-start. The bike's modified, thunderous pipes echoed inside the garage.

Adrenaline fueled by rage coursed through me as I backed into the street.

Yanking hard on the throttle, my motorcycle rocketed off the pavement. My bike was at full acceleration by the time I passed my friend Mike's house only three doors away.

A car came toward me, and as I sped forward, the scene went slow motion. In the middle of our narrow street, the car seemed to stand still. The driver may have braked at the sight of a motorcycle approaching full-bore.

My bike flew to meet it head-on, closer and closer to impact. My angered grip kept the throttle pulled back.

I detected Mike on the periphery, standing at his driveway. He grasped his head, waiting for the impending crash.

Seconds divided into split seconds.

The tarnish of the vehicle's chrome grill came into clear view. The car's headlights grew larger; the grooved lines of the glass lenses came into sharp focus.

My senses broke down my options, and in a blink in time, I leaned left to swerve past the car, roaring to safety in the narrow path between the car and another parked vehicle.

I cruised the city streets, mulling the power of anger. Anger gave me strength and courage, heightening my vision, reactions, and hearing. It was like having superpowers. Rage kept me secure, dwelling inside me at the ready to make people back down when they saw my eyes.

After a while, I returned and stopped at Mike's house.

"Man, what happened?" he asked. "All of a sudden I look up and you're heading full speed at a car." He held his hands six inches apart. "You were this close to hitting it. I thought you were dust."

"I was pissed off about something," I said matter-of-factly. "That's all. It wasn't nothing."

23

Dad, Eye to Eye

"**D**ogpile!" **the neighborhood** kids, two doors away, caught my attention. They had converged at the side yard between the Garcia's and Patterson's houses, creating pancake layers of arms and legs amid whoops and giggles.

In the early evening after suppertime, I leaned against Mrs. Rucker's car parked in the driveway. Chuck was in the house, and I stayed outside waiting for friends to show. I had drained my fifth beer and considered finishing the six-pack. My mood was content and lighthearted.

When the kids gathered for the next round, I walked toward them.

"Dogpile!" someone shouted. I broke into a sprint, timing my arrival to be the last on top.

"Dogpile!" I yelled, stretching my arms and legs outward in flight. My surprise appearance would add to the fun.

The pile of kids passed underneath me as I overshot the mark.

Aquamarine-colored sheet metal filled my vision, and my arms folded to the elbow on impact at the quarter panel of Mr. Patterson's truck, behind the front wheel well. My head sounded a loud bang as it smacked the GMC truck.

In seconds, I picked myself up off the ground and marveled at the pain-dampening effects of alcohol.

"You're bleeding!" A boy half my size ran to me, his eyes focused on the top of my head.

"I am?"

When I touched my forehead, bright red covered my fingertips. Another touch at my hairline confirmed a sizable gash.

I hurried to the bathroom at Chuck's house.

With one hand holding hair away from the wound, and another grasping a swath of toilet paper, I dabbed at it. I examined the laceration in the mirror, glad it had clotted.

Am I plastered or what? I considered my injury a product of too much to drink.

The crimson-colored flesh tear matched the red streaks that twisted through my eyes like a Rand McNally map. It was the first time I beheld myself while intoxicated.

My father's eyes seemed to stare back at me. Startled, I stepped away, but returned to my reflection and looked again.

Dad's familiar bloodshot eyes peered back. How could this be? I hadn't seen Dad drink since we moved. In San Jose, there always seemed to be a can of Hamm's or Olympia in the icebox. In Milpitas, there were no beers in the refrigerator.

My memory rolled tape like a home movie. Dad spent a lot of time in his bedroom. When I walked by his open door, sometimes he lay in bed watching TV. Other times, he sat in his easy chair smoking a cigar. Every so often, he sat in the dark, and I likened it to listening for a bear's breathing at a cave entrance.

Sometimes he charged out of his room like a junkyard dog and unleashed his fury. He usually blew up about something that never seemed to be about anything. He seemed to stew in his thoughts and then come out of his bedroom to vent his frustrations and resentments.

Despite little evidence, Dad had the makings of a closet drinker. He never staggered like a lurching drunk. He didn't slur his words, and he never smelled of alcohol.

I realized his eyes were probably drunken red, just as mine were now.

The next morning, my mind nudged me to fill in the blanks. I went to the garage to look for something I hadn't given much thought to before—empty liquor bottles.

They stood out like flashing lights. One was an empty decanter, a

Christmas gift from the neighbor next door. In previous months, it had been displayed unopened on a kitchen shelf. Now it sat without contents next to a jar of carpenter nails.

A bottle of vodka sat on another shelf. I picked it up, its contents now nothing but air. From time to time, other bottles had made their way to the garage. What was the purpose of keeping them? Was it some kind of way station before their final trash-can destination?

Years later, when I lived in my own place, it struck me that I did something similar to Dad. I displayed empty liquor bottles as decorations on my kitchen counter. Sometimes they were like souvenirs, reminiscent of good times. Did Dad do the same—hold bottles in the garage to remind him of former times? Maybe holding on to them was a message to his family that he couldn't help himself.

As a youth, I couldn't comprehend why Dad always seemed to be angry, rarely happy. He didn't talk about his life in the Philippines or the US except in bits and pieces. Maybe there were events in his past that drove him to drink.

Looking back, his drinking in secret was like throwing gasoline on a fire.

24

Graduation

Late in the fall semester of my senior year, we reviewed our transcripts in homeroom to make sure we were on track to graduate in the spring. I discovered that if I passed my current classes, I'd have enough units to graduate midterm.

I'd known many of my classmates since elementary school, but I wasn't close to any. I'd miss the senior ball, same as the junior prom. I didn't ask anyone to go because I wasn't part of the mainstream crowd. I didn't know those formals were a big deal.

Despite growing up with a mother and two older sisters, I didn't know how to talk to girls either. Missing the senior ball meant I could avoid awkward feelings and questions.

I was ready to leave. Gone would be the days of feeling self-conscious in high school, of sitting alone believing I was the only one who didn't have friends, of not belonging anywhere.

My midterm graduation application required obtaining my teachers' signatures and their projections of my final semester grade. With each letter grade I received, excitement over my imminent departure grew.

At break, Coach Malchow walked toward the locker rooms. His was my last signature to acquire.

"Coach! Hey, Coach," I yelled. My voice echoed through the breezeway.

He turned around. A swaying ring full of keys hooked on his belt jingled to a stop.

"Yeah, Cruz."

With my arm outstretched and paperwork in hand, I rushed over.

"I'm graduating midterm," I said. In Coach Malchow's classes, I had demonstrated tennis strokes and basketball skills to the students. I sometimes led the class in stretching and warm-up exercises. In most units, I performed above average and hustled 100 percent of the time. My final grade would be an easy A.

After jotting my grade and scribbling his signature, he handed me my grade report. Amid the Cs and one B from other teachers, I looked for my A grade. On the line following his name, I did a double take. It looked like an F. He must've left off the right leg of my A.

"That's for not going out," he said. His tone sounded confrontational.

More incredulous than angered, I glared at him. But I remained silent and pretended it didn't bother me. In my mind, I knew where he could stick his F.

We turned away without another word.

I puzzled about a coach who took my lack of joining sports so personally. I had no desire to explain my home life, which prevented my participating in sports. He probably wouldn't understand anyway. He only cared about fielding successful teams.

Would I need to return the next semester just for a PE class? Maybe I could petition or appeal to do extra credit.

The administration office bustled with students voicing their needs and concerns. Behind the front counter, secretaries answered phone calls from parents about attendance and schedules. At a side counter, I waited for the registrar with my hands clasped over my final grade report as if it were a ticket to a Led Zeppelin concert.

From across the room, a woman holding a file folder walked toward me. Her gait was purposeful, striding in a way many do when they're too busy. As she approached, she smiled pleasantly. I was thankful she hadn't yet had her day's fill of excitable teenagers. Perhaps as a graduating senior, I deserved adult-like respect.

Graduation

"I got an F in PE," I said when I handed her my report.

Unruffled, she opened the file folder containing my school records. She penciled a few numbers on the outside, then raised her head to meet my eyes. "You have enough units to graduate anyway," she said.

"Oh," I said. "That's good. Thanks." I had clutched the counter's edge, expecting instructions about how to make up the failing grade.

"We'll send a confirmation letter to your home. It'll contain information about the graduation ceremony and getting your yearbook. Congratulations on graduating!"

My face flushed with the understanding that my high school career would indeed finish early. I thanked her.

Coach Malchow wouldn't get a win by holding up my midterm graduation. I strolled away content in knowing that.

In the spring, when word got around that I had finished high school, a few Winchell's Donuts managers in San Jose invited me to work additional hours. I had been a part-time employee in Milpitas since I was a sophomore. I ended up dividing my week between three stores.

Fritz, the manager of a small shop in east San Jose, took me under his wing. He showed me his tricks of the trade to become more efficient and to curb expenses.

"Some managers start out here and then move on to bigger shops," he said. "This could be your shop. I'm retiring soon." In the early morning hours before the store's opening, his announcement caught me by surprise.

Confident I could run my own shop, I simply needed to learn how to keep the books and hire reliable staff. The orange Datsun 240Z I'd recently test-driven streaked through my memory. I could afford it with manager pay.

The mound of dough resembled a beige-colored balloon. I tossed flour on it, and a cloud of white dust lingered in the air before falling over the cutting board.

"Fritz, why you retiring?"

He gazed at the floor.

"My health is not so good. After thirty years of inhaling flour, I have a hard time breathing."

"Oh, I'm sorry to hear that."

I pushed the rolling pin over the dough, leveling it to a thickness suitable for jelly-filled donuts. I didn't envision a future life where I struggled for air, girl-catching sports car or not. A slideshow in my mind clicked forward a frame.

Maybe I could succeed in college.

———

After another early morning shift at the donut shop, I arrived home for lunch. I sat at the kitchen table while Mom prepared the meal. I had changed clothes and would help Dad in the backyard. Dad milled about.

"Yes sir, that's good you have a job. Idle hands are the devil's playground," he said. I didn't let on that at the age of eighteen, I was a top prospect to run my own store. I didn't want to provide him ammunition for criticism. He went out to the garage.

Mom, as usual, said nothing. She pushed a plate of steaming rice, vegetables, and chicken in front of me.

"I've decided to go to college," I said, declaring it more to myself than to Mom. I wanted to hear me say it and feel convinced. I expected her to remain silent.

"I don't care," she said in a sharp tone. "As long as you pay the rent." She frowned as if I'd cursed at her.

Even though she was married to Dad, I couldn't believe she could be so cold to me.

My lunch became tasteless.

While I was growing up, she'd spoken to me just a handful of times. This was one of them.

My baking donuts continued to pay my share of the rent.

In the fall, I enrolled in classes at San Jose City College.

25

A Rash Discovery

A sky-blue, half-sheet flyer tacked to a kiosk rustled in the breeze and caught my attention. It read: *Problems? Worries? Concerns? Talk to a Counselor Intern. Confidential.*

Perhaps I qualified. At age eighteen, I didn't know what I wanted to do with my life. I felt trapped at home because I didn't earn enough money at the donut shop to move out. I had few friends. And my skin disorder lingered.

In the fall of 1975, I enrolled in three classes at San Jose City College to gauge my interest in higher education. Although I survived high school with a C average, almost on purpose, I knew I could do much better. Yet I wasn't sure student life was for me. Maybe the best thing was to find a full-time job.

My coping mechanisms were still in place. With friends, I drank myself into oblivion or smoked dope into an uncaring high, never letting on about my family troubles. On my motorcycle, I was an untouchable bird in flight. When I played sports, I concentrated solely on the arc of my basketball shot or the spin of the tennis ball.

Writing my thoughts and feelings in a journal also provided release. A few times I wrote things in all capital letters, like, "WHY IS LIFE SO UNFAIR?" Sometimes, swear words littered the pages when I corralled feelings of sadness, helplessness, and pessimism. Most of the time, I tried to make sense of my life.

Maybe it would be good to talk to someone trained to help me understand the catastrophe of my upbringing.

John reclined in his office chair. Slender and tall, possibly ten years older than I, he had a short beard and combed his dirty-blond hair to the side. His demeanor was calm, and he smiled. But as with everyone, I regarded him cautiously.

"Hi, Pete," he said. "What brings you in?"

I didn't know specifically what brought me in. I only knew my entire life had been pain, problems, and worries.

"I'm not sure," I replied, my voice unsteady. Anxiety darted inside my stomach like bees around a hive. I found it difficult to trust anyone, and John was a complete stranger.

"It's okay," he said softly. "Take your time." His facial expression conveyed kindness.

"The flyer said I could talk to a counselor about my problems. I've never done anything like that."

"You're in the right place. You can talk about things as much as you want or as little. I'm here for you." He gave a slight smile and sat patiently.

"I have a lot of problems, most of them probably because of a bad home life."

"Hmm. I see." He waited for me to continue.

My personal problems outweighed my need to remain behind my self-imposed walls. And I had nothing to lose. So for the first time, I confided in someone. Each passing week, I talked more about how I grew up. I expressed my feelings of unhappiness. Mostly I spoke about my father.

Even when I didn't come away with any particular insights, it felt good to talk to someone who listened without judgment or criticism.

One day it was time to divulge one of my biggest concerns.

I pulled my sleeve to the elbow, revealing an open wound, but partially healed.

"I've had this skin condition since I was a sophomore in high school. A lot of the spots have closed, but some haven't. The doctors call it eczema, but I don't think they really know."

He looked closely. "Hmm. I know you're not allowed to express your feelings in front of your dad. The next time he gets angry at you, let me know how you feel. Tell me what your body is going through."

I hadn't paid attention to what my body was going through when enduring Dad's fits of rage.

I grew curious about what effects Dad's tirades might have on my body.

It didn't take long to get an answer.

That afternoon, I attached damp laundry to a hanger with clothespins, and hoisted the hanger to the ceiling for drying. A wooden pole with two nails hammered into its end in a V configuration held the hanger in place.

As I tried to hook a full hanger onto a nail on the side of a ceiling beam, it fell. The slight plop on the linoleum floor sounded an alert to Dad in the kitchen.

"Dammit!" he screamed. "What's wrong with you? What are you? Stupid?" I braced for an onrush of slaps, kicks, or the drawing of his belt. Instead, his verbal onslaught continued like torrential rain.

My stomach churned and my body went limp under his withering accusations. Nausea and weakness were soon replaced by intense frustration and resentment. His unfair indictments gave way to swirling anger.

My body felt engulfed in flames. I couldn't release my frustrations and resentment. I was "Johnny Storm, the Human Torch," in *The Fantastic Four* comic books. When time for battle came, he cried, "Flame On!"

My body was in battle—one I didn't ask for. Dad's actions had ignited an inferno within me.

As always, I knew that if Dad sensed displeasure, further torment would befall me. So I kept my feelings bottled up.

With deliberate care, I picked up the clothes and rehung them, wary of Dad's every move.

"It felt like my blood was boiling," I said to John during our next session. "I get so angry at the way my dad treats me, but I can't scream or throw things or he'll get madder."

"It sounds like you haven't the means to release your emotions. Have you heard of psychosomatic illness?"

"No." It didn't sound good.

"It literally means mind-body illness. What goes on in your mind can manifest itself in your body. It's like a stress headache." He explained it, and I understood.

"In your case, it could be that your unexpressed emotions need release at an extreme level and that it has affected your skin in a bad way."

"That makes a lot of sense." I imagined my body as the world, with volcanoes erupting at different parts.

"In our next session, we can look at ways for you to express anger, perhaps journaling or meditation exercises."

John had uncovered the key. In subsequent visits, we worked on methods to release my pent-up anger and frustrations. My body's natural healing processes were gradually able to take over. Weekly counseling visits provided a mental outlet. I felt more in control of my life and my body. And for the most part, many of my skin's problem areas healed.

For the remaining mental and physical healing to take place, it became clear that I needed to leave home.

26

Future Focus

"**Hey, Elena!**" **My** city college teacher excitedly spoke into the phone. "This is Lonnie calling from San Jose. I have someone here in my office I think you'll like. His name is Pete Cruz. He's a very thoughtful and aware young man."

I didn't know what to think. I wasn't used to an adult speaking highly of me and then calling someone on my behalf.

Mr. Highsmith was my career planning instructor. He said that despite my C average in high school, he knew of a program that helped students from low-income, disadvantaged backgrounds attend a four-year college. Arrangements were made for me to visit California State University, Sacramento, in the next month.

My childhood friend, Russell, and I left on a road trip unlike others we'd taken. Normally we drove somewhere, took in the sights, loitered and lingered, smoked weed, scoped out the girls, and returned home.

"I knew you had it in you, Pete. You were always the smartest of all of us." Russell's late model Chevy Camaro powered north on Interstate 5. We talked animatedly about the possibility of my becoming a college student.

Ahead of us, the prominent CSU, Sacramento sign stood proudly before this institution of higher learning. The entranceway opened to tall evergreens and fir trees. I stared wide-eyed at the different buildings. We slowed to gawk at the miniature Golden Gate pedestrian bridge spanning the American River before parking on a graveled lot on the edge of campus.

In the admissions office, I was introduced to Elena, the director of the Educational Opportunity Program (EOP). "Lonnie was a student here," she said. "He doesn't call me often, but when he does, I listen. He sees something in you."

Living up to expectations seemed like a burden. I didn't know how to take the endorsement.

A young Japanese woman strolled in and introduced herself as Satsuki, one of the counselors. She moved in a gentle but determined manner. She walked me to another room and instructed me to write an essay about my background and why I wanted to attend college. The EOP staff would review my application paperwork, my test results, and my essay.

After I completed the final essay, Russell and I sat outside on a bench. It was lunchtime, and he seemed weary from waiting so long. He didn't complain, and was still encouraging me about my prospects to attend a university. None of our friends cared about going to college.

Eventually Satsuki came out and took a seat next to me. She calmly looked me in the eye and said, "All the paperwork you've completed, from the tests you took to the essay you wrote, gives us a picture of whether you exhibit potential to be a successful student."

I listened intently.

"Pete, we believe you fit that picture of success," she said. "We'd like you to come to this school."

My throat constricted, and I took in a small breath. Russell grinned as if he were let in on an inside joke. My mind clattered from equal parts disbelief and delight.

"You're not going to be left alone. We'll assign you a counselor, as well as a peer advisor, to guide you through your course selections and to help you adjust to campus life. We'll provide you a financial-aid package to help pay for your books and fees."

"Looks like I'm moving," I nodded to Russell.

"Way to go, man. Congratulations!"

My future came into view. No longer would I return home each day with knots in my stomach. Soon I'd be out from under Dad's reign.

Future Focus

Clothes lay about my bed in carefully formed piles as I considered how to fit them into a single suitcase. I'd soon be leaving for the spring 1976 semester at California State University, Sacramento—Sac State.

My ears perked up when I heard Dad approach. I lowered my head and continued to pack, hoping he'd walk to the bathroom at the end of the hallway. Instead, he stopped and leaned against the doorframe. As always, I feared the worst, certain he'd rifle through my belongings and tell me what I wasn't allowed to take. My breathing became shallow. Maybe he'd bellow something unpredictable.

"That reminds me of my travels. I got lots of practice packing. Sometimes we had no notice we had to leave. We followed the crops from oranges in Visalia to apples in Washington."

Until then, my frame of reference to orchards was as a small boy picking cherries in San Jose. I never knew that for Dad, farm work was a way of life.

Even at nineteen, I'd never held a conversation with Dad. Although I wanted to find out more about his itinerant farm life, I remained silent, careful that anything I said could set him off.

"There was a time in Watsonville," he continued. Watsonville was a sleepy town on the way to Monterey from Santa Cruz. I'd been on many outings in that area with friends—drinking, smoking, and meeting girls.

"I was walking across the street when some white guy screamed at me, 'Hey, you brown monkey! Get out of here!' We got into a big fight because of that. We had to leave right way."

Dad seemed softer, pensive, not the fuming Dad I was used to. I paused my packing to steal a glance at him, holding on to each word like a prized possession. For the first time, I didn't view him through lenses of fear and caution.

What must it have been like for him to be assaulted because of his race? I recalled the time my friends and I crashed a house party in San Jose. The host assailed me with derogatory, hurtful terms about Chinks, Nips, and Japs.

It was his party, attended by his friends. I had come with a handful of my buddies. We left, deciding to confront the host when there were even numbers between his friends and mine. A week later, I knocked on his door with my friends Dirk and Mike, and invited him to meet me with two of his. Without a word, he shut the door, and I never saw him again.

Dad fled a town I regarded as unimportant. I packed to travel north for a promising future. But he'd hurriedly gathered his things to escape violence after battling to get respect from those who judged him based on skin color.

Had I discovered a source of his ceaseless anger?

27

A Moving Experience

"**I'm gonna go** now," I announced to Dad in my best may-I-be-excused manner.

"Okay," he replied. His tone was indifferent and he turned away.

My parents didn't walk me to my car or stand at the doorway to wave goodbye. No moist-eyed "Good luck" or "We'll miss you" or "We're proud of you." No prolonged hugs or faltering emotion-filled voices.

Not that I expected any of that.

Father-son communication always came with churned stomach acids and on-edge fear.

Mother-son communication lacked any connection.

I was fine with receiving only an "Okay" when I departed. After all, I left home without getting kicked out. Others had fled in desperation.

Despite Dad's severe manner, he gave me his car, my first car, a 1969 Chevrolet Impala with a powerful 327-cubic-inch V8 engine, white tonneau roof, matching vinyl seats, royal blue body paint, and a wood-grained dashboard. His gift became my getaway vehicle.

As the distance lengthened from Milpitas, open road and silence gave way to a pensive mood. I drove not so much relieved to escape, but satisfied I'd exited on what I believed were my own terms.

At dinnertime, the residence hall community gathered at the Dining Commons. The Commons served dinner only between five and seven o'clock. Because meals were part of my financial-aid package, this trapped me into eating with everyone else. I had little money to go off campus for a fast-food meal.

I wrestled with extreme fear and anxiety around new people and places, much as I did when going to a new school or classroom as a boy.

Rows of tables were filled with students chatting and laughing with each other. Since I had enrolled midyear, it appeared that everyone already enjoyed established relationships. With nowhere to hide, I sat by myself. A sandwich board in my mind advertised me as "Awkward New Student with No Friends."

My food tasted bland and I hung my head. The din of conversations faded to background noise—the same as when I sat alone against a slat-wood fence during second-grade recess.

At one of the long, rectangular tables across from me, I recognized a student who lived on my floor. He engaged in animated conversation with a guy next to him. He flailed his arms to make his point, like a hawk about to take flight.

Some of the guys at the table appeared to scrutinize me. Others glanced at me and turned away when I looked back. I steeled myself for a coming threat.

The guy I recognized grinned and said, "Hey, Pete, there's room over here if you'd like to join us."

"Huh?" I returned a reluctant smile and got up slowly to begin a heavy-footed walk to his table.

"My name's Tom." Gangly, with a sharp nose and thin, blond hair, he shook my hand.

"Have a seat." The guy next to him gestured to an open chair. "My name's Cameron. People call me 'Cam' for short, you know, like the engine part?"

Cam clutched my hand in a strong handshake. He was a big, muscular dude, with beachboy looks. Despite the winter months, he must've seen his share of tanning booths. I was sure every female in the place fawned over him.

Tom seemed to be the group spokesman, and Cam's welcome seemed to voice his approval to the others lining the table.

To my surprise, every guy there lived on my floor. Each waved and introduced himself—the residents of Sutter Hall, third floor.

In the dorms, there was always something to do and someone to do it with. One student said, "This is just like a resort. There are different activities to get involved with, opportunities for socializing, and beautiful women walking around." My head swerved to appraise a passing co-ed. "The problem is classes get in the way."

Classes took some getting used to. Satsuki, my EOP counselor, made sure I'd enrolled in a combination of solid and soft classes, meaning some classes were more demanding than others.

The syllabus, an unknown concept to me, required careful under-standing of tasks, deadlines, and grading. My first English assignment was due in two days. In my government course, chapters needed to be read before every meeting. When each professor emphasized the coursework, I gulped. *Don't they know I have other classes?*

For one of my electives, I enrolled in "Filipino-American Experience." I was surprised such a class existed. Were there enough Filipinos to hold a class? In Milpitas, there were only three Filipino families I knew of. As it turned out, many students hailed from large Filipino communities in Stockton and Vallejo, cities sixty and ninety minutes from Sacramento.

The class helped fill a cultural void in my self-identity. I learned that the educational system in the Philippines is a replica of that in the United States, and that English has been taught in grade school since after the US liberated the Philippines from Spain's four-hundred-year rule. As a result of the Spanish conquest, my surname, Cruz, had probably been changed from a native Filipino last name.

On the first day of class, while flipping through my textbook, I froze on a page showing a black-and-white photo of Filipino men posing in front of a storefront. The chapter was titled, "The Watsonville Riots." It said fights broke out when an angry white man shouted, "Hey, you brown monkey!" to a Filipino man crossing the street.

I stared at the sentence, bringing it into sharp focus like a camera zooming in on a subject. Just a week earlier while I packed for school, Dad had recalled the exact same Watsonville incident involving him—and the same words.

In the 1930s, Filipino laborers arrived in the US in large numbers to work the fields. Immigration laws limited Filipino women's entry to a one-to-fifteen ratio. Hostilities arose when young Filipino men intermingled with white women. The riots lasted for several days, resulting in the death of a Filipino man.

Though at the time Dad was an immigrant in his early twenties, I believe he arrived with his fiery, prideful anger in place. He wouldn't have let a racial insult pass. It seemed more than coincidence that he was the target of the racial epithet cited in my textbook.

At my desk, I stayed silent about my findings. I didn't want any attention my discovery could bring. The students would've asked questions to which I had no answers. My professor might've invited my father to the classroom.

It wasn't as if I could call or visit Dad with textbook in hand and ask, "Was that you?"

I didn't need to ask. I knew the answer.

28

Meeting Margaret

In the Filipino-American Experience class taught by Maxi, I had become the teaching assistant during the second semester of my junior year. She also invited me to become involved with the Filipino community. The Philippine National Day (PND) committee convened in an old office building in South Sacramento. PND commemorates the declaration of Philippine independence from Spain in 1898.

People on "Filipino time" gradually sauntered in. Thirty minutes after the scheduled start, Maxi called us to order.

The other participants were older, except for one girl at the opposite corner of the table. Everyone appeared to know each other from past activities.

I always had difficulty meeting new people in new settings. I breathed deeply, knowing no other way to quiet my nerves.

Maxi stepped behind each member's chair for introductions, stating names, occupations, and past civic experience. Their information hardly registered with me because of apprehension at my own introduction.

Maxi stood behind the girl at the opposite corner.

"This is Margaret," Maxi said. "She's our university representative from Sac State, as is Pete Cruz."

Margaret wore a sleeveless dress with white flower designs on a blue background. Her silky black hair hung in front of her shoulders. Demure brown eyes batted long lashes when she glanced at me. Full lips smiled before she returned to face forward.

Throughout the meeting, I tried to stay on topic, taking notes of my assignments while I peeked at Margaret. Getting to know her better became my new priority.

The meeting concluded too soon. As members stood to leave and said, "Nice to meet you," I moved toward Margaret, irresistibly drawn but as skittish as a hamster on a wheel.

She turned to me.

"So you go to Sac State?" I said.

"Yeah, I do."

"What year are you?"

"I'm a sophomore."

"I'm a junior," I said. "What's your major?"

"I'm thinking of going into sociology." Her deep brown eyes made my heart skip a beat. "How about you?"

"I'm an English major." I was thankful for having learned rote conversation starters. Otherwise, my unease would've been obvious.

"Nice to meet you," I said. "I'll see you next meeting or maybe on campus." I decided to quit before I became desperate for other conversation topics.

"Okay," she said. Her smile captivated me.

I floated to my car, oblivious to the time of day or my next destination.

My American Literature professor droned endlessly about *Moby Dick*, but I may as well have been out to sea. My thoughts were only on Margaret.

I broke myself away from my daydreams and turned to my blank binder paper. I missed several points the professor had made. He continued to jot words on the chalkboard, but I still couldn't connect them to the lesson.

For the next two weeks, I planted myself on a bench adjacent to the entrance of the sociology building because sociology was Margaret's major. I looked for every Filipina with hair flowing past her shoulders, hoping it'd be her. She never happened by.

I looked forward to the next PND meeting.

Meeting Margaret

A few people were at the conference table when I entered. Margaret sat at the same corner as before.

Maxi stood nearby and smiled at me, but continued her conversation with another member.

When I stepped toward Margaret, nervousness threatened to derail me, but our eyes met and she smiled. I continued forward and forced myself to upturn the sides of my mouth because smiling for me was as unnatural as writing my name with my opposite hand.

"Hi, Margaret," I said. Anxiety mushroomed. "Is anyone sitting here?" I motioned to the seat next to her, hoping my nerves would settle if I sat.

"No, nobody. You can sit there."

"How are your classes?" I kept with safe subjects.

"They're good," she said. "I'm not too busy before midterms." She didn't provide me with one-word answers—a good sign.

"Are you at school much?" I asked, and thought of how much time I'd wasted waiting outside the sociology building.

"Three days, maybe more if I need to use the library. How about you?" She asked about me!

During the meeting, I tried to listen to everyone and not be obvious in my attraction to Margaret. I was aware of her every movement, every scribble of her pencil. Her perfume had the fragrance of flowers. I was as helpless as Pepé Le Pew pining for Penelope Pussycat—and just as looney.

The meeting adjourned an hour later, and I turned to Margaret for my moment of truth.

"Hey, do you want to meet on campus?" I hoped I didn't sound as if I were pleading. "We could meet at the Student Union for a Coke. Or we could study together."

She smiled. I braced myself for rejection and stood to gather my things.

"Yeah, I'd like that. Do you want my phone number?"

I couldn't believe it.

Trying my best to conceal my joy, I jotted her number in the margin of my meeting notes.

"I'll talk to you later." I exited in brisk fashion, not wanting to give her time to change her mind or come up with excuses.

Outside in the cool night air, excitement washed over me like waves on a beach.

Eagerness mingled with anxiety as I peered at every student browsing the Sac State library bookshelves. My spiral notebook and backpack lay on the coffee table.

I glimpsed at my watch every two minutes.

At ten minutes before the hour, doubt and insecurity visited. I considered the time it'd take her to drive from the South Area. Maybe she'd changed her mind. Maybe she didn't like me after all. Maybe she got a flat tire on the way over. Why was I so stupid to think anyone could like me or that anything good could happen in my life?

At seven o'clock, my body was like a washing machine; the paddles churned gray-water anxiety side to side. I held my arms to my stomach, uncomfortable, unable to turn the agitator off.

At five minutes after seven, I became certain she wouldn't show. I was helpless to do anything about it. I'd be a dejected and rejected mess for the next few days. Despite regular sessions at the campus counseling center, I'd not yet connected my anxiety to abandonment issues.

My ears perked at another student hiking through the book stacks. I anticipated he or she would give me an apathetic look, another reminder no one cared about me. I tilted my head to see who approached.

Margaret appeared in front of me. Her eyes sparkled when she saw me.

"Hi," she said. "I had to park at the temp buildings by Maxi's office. Otherwise, I would've been here sooner." She smiled broadly.

Relief and contentment washed over me.

Although students randomly walked by, it seemed like just her and me in the world. We talked about our lives, our families, our likes and dislikes, and our needs and desires. Time seemed at a standstill.

"It's almost ten-thirty," I said, aware that no one had strolled by in quite a while. "We should probably go. The library closes at eleven."

"Yeah, it's late," she said. "I don't want to disturb my roommates."

I rose and hoisted my backpack over my shoulder.

She gathered her belongings from the table and turned to me. A warm smile crested her face.

Grasping her hand seemed a natural gesture given our mutual attraction. Instead of withdrawing, she squeezed my hand as we stepped toward the exit.

The crisp, cool evening air made for a brisk walk to her car. The quietness of the campus amplified our voices—a distinct departure from daytime hours when thousands of students moved about.

We stopped at her car. The parking area was dimly lit, except for some lighting from distant lampposts. No one seemed to be around. A full moon illuminated our surroundings. Despite the chill air, there was an inner glow between us. We still held hands.

"Drive safely," I said. "I want to see you again."

"I will," she said, smiling. "You'll see me again."

I pulled her closer to me. She offered no resistance when I encircled her with my arms. I pressed my lips to hers. I drew back to judge her reaction. She returned my gaze, content and happy. Below her long lashes, her deep brown eyes reflected joy.

"See you tomorrow on campus?"

"I'm looking forward to it, and I haven't even left yet."

Margaret and I became a couple. She was my first official girlfriend ever.

First love is the deepest, I'd heard. It was also the sweetest and the most innocent.

29

Love Not Lasting

Margaret filled a vast emptiness inside of me. I had finally found someone who cared about me, appreciated me, and loved me. We walked proudly hand in hand on campus, stopped among friends, excited to introduce ourselves as a couple. Like daffodils in spring, our relationship blossomed.

As we crossed an expanse of lawn fronting the library quad, clouds like puffs of cotton dotted the blue sky on a breezeless day. We wandered toward the English and sociology buildings for our next classes.

"There's Rolando!" Margaret cried. She jerked my hand and I stopped in place like a reined-in horse.

I looked in the direction of her turned head.

"Who's that?" I asked.

"Rolando! Hey, Rollie!" she shouted without replying to me. She fully extended her arm and waved as if flagging a cab on a busy street.

My eyes pinpointed the object of her attention. Rolando was a slender, tall guy with dark features.

He turned his head when Margaret yelled louder. His eyes enlarged to silver-dollar size and his mouth broadened to a grin.

As Margaret stood on her tiptoes waving, I became aware of the sun gleaming across her shapely bronze legs.

My chest and abdomen constricted as fear exploded with a deepening realization—my girlfriend was a surefire attraction to the opposite sex.

Rolando stepped on the grassy turf and walked toward us.

Margaret halted our progress to class when she saw Rolando, meaning he was important enough to stop for. Her need to shout and wave to get his attention meant she liked him a lot. He was taller than I. His smile and casual stride suggested confidence.

My conclusion: he could take Margaret away from me.

My jaw clenched as he approached. I waited next to Margaret. My stomach whirled like a blender with a broken off button.

"Hi, Margaret!" he said. He wrapped his long arms around her.

"Hi, Rolando!" She spun to me, away from his grasp.

Rolando turned to appraise me and smiled.

"I want you to meet . . ." Margaret continued.

I glared at Rolando and snorted like a wild bull.

With a short wave of my hand, I dismissed him.

Rolando's eyes narrowed to nickel size; his smile vanished. My behavior shocked and confused him. He looked to Margaret for an out.

I turned my back to him.

"Pete, what's wrong?" Margaret's voice registered the same confounded surprise. "I'm sorry, Rolando. You better go."

"I'm sorry," Rolando said in a muted voice.

After he left, I lowered my head in shame and stared at the green grass. I felt small enough to hide behind each blade.

"Hey. Hey, it's me. Look at me. I'm right here." Margaret positioned herself in front of me. She held her hands to the sides of my face, gently lifting my head so I could see her. Her eyes, inches from mine, expressed deep concern and care.

"I don't know what happened, but you don't have to worry. He's just a friend. I only wanted you to meet him." She kept her hands around my face so I wouldn't avert my gaze. "I love you," she said. "There's only you. You're my boyfriend."

Trying to blink away the increasing moisture in my eyes, I wanted to cry but couldn't. Students passed behind her with curiosity on their faces.

"I'm so sorry," I said, my voice barely audible. "I don't know. I couldn't help it." I pressed my lips together tighter, hoping to trap the ugliness inside. Shame overwhelmed me.

"It's okay. You don't have to talk now," Margaret said. "Are you ready to go to class?"

"Yeah." I brushed tears from my eyes.

Margaret's smile conveyed encouragement. Kindness reflected from her eyes. She grasped my upper arm with her two hands and rested her head against my shoulder. We walked away in silence.

I didn't deserve her. I was astonished that she still wanted to be with me.

―――――――――

Late in the fall, darkness descended over Interstate 680 after our return trip from visiting my parents. Milpitas receded in the rearview mirror as we approached the hills above Fremont.

"I don't think your dad's a bad person," Margaret said. "I think you should give him a break."

She faced me with her back partially against the passenger seat and the door. I couldn't comprehend what she had just said.

"He never gave me a break."

"That doesn't mean you can't give him one." Her statement bore into me accusingly, as if I were the one at fault in my most sensitive subject.

"How can you say that?" My internal heat index shot upward. "You don't understand. Every day he yelled at me or hit me. He never had anything good to say about me. I grew up in constant fear."

"People change. In the two times I've met him, he's been nice to me. You should forgive him. I think he'd be open to that."

"No!" My body shuddered as my voice trembled. "You have no idea. You don't know what you're talking about." The back of my neck rose in temperature. "Yes, he's nice to you. How someone acts in public can be a lot different than behind closed doors."

She sat with her arms folded.

The way I saw it, Margaret had dismissed my feelings as unreal, my thoughts as meaningless. I took it as betrayal. I actually wanted to be home and away from her. My jaw set in place like hardened concrete. I ground my teeth. I snorted. Nothing more to say.

Wiping sweaty hands on my pant legs to get a better hold of the steering wheel, I pushed my foot on the accelerator. We hurtled through the mountainous highway as I weaved between cars that seemed at a standstill.

The cars in the fast lane were too slow. I hugged their bumpers until each one moved out of the way. Those unwilling to change lanes received a dose of my high beams.

Margaret pressed against her seat. Dread riddled her face as we charged headlong behind each car until it moved out of my way. She gaped at me, her eyes wide open in disbelief. Her bottom lip quivered as my rage from a lifetime of abuse played itself out in her car.

Finally, we arrived in Sacramento. I parked at her apartment and handed her keys to her.

"I'm gonna go now," I said. Still hurt, I sought to protect the child within me who'd never been looked after. "We should probably break up."

She nodded, her expression forlorn and helpless.

Weeks later, in the early evening, I went to Margaret's apartment to pick up belongings I'd left there. Our conversation was stilted, careful, and carried a sad air of finality. In the past, she'd taken me back after angry outbursts at her and others, but this last experience proved insurmountable. She'd witnessed the total extent of my full-blown rage, which put her safety at risk.

I descended her stairwell a final time. My footfalls echoed between apartment units.

On the path to the parking lot, each lamppost I passed cast my shadow against exterior walls.

Alone again.

30

From Loner to Leader

"**Al's not going** to be here today to teach his class. You'll have to do it," Ricardo, an EOP counselor, said. He was calm and matter-of-fact.

"What? Me?" I gawked at him.

"He's got a family emergency. He won't be back in time."

"Should we cancel?"

"No, our contract doesn't allow that."

"Can someone else teach it?"

"No, you're his TA. You have to cover for him."

"I may be his teaching assistant, but I've never taught a class by myself." I stammered and held my hand to my chest, afraid my heart would pop out.

"You'll think of something. That's why Al picked you to be his TA," Ricardo said, as if he were commenting on the weather.

The first week of the fall semester of my senior year had begun two days earlier. I stood at the chalkboard waiting for the clock's second hand to click on twelve, signifying ten o'clock sharp.

First-year students settled into their seats, readying for the start of "Strategies of Learning," an interdisciplinary course that provided instruction in study skills, time management, and resources for academic and social success.

In an effort to hold myself together, I clasped my hands and pasted a smile on my face. I tried not to glance about like a wild-eyed squirrel.

The merciless, audible click of the second hand ticked at ten o'clock like the grim reaper's swing of his scythe.

"Good morning, class," I began. "Mr. Striplen won't be here today. I have the opportunity to teach this class for the next fifty minutes."

One minute had elapsed when I glanced at the clock. How was I going to get through the other forty-nine? I surveyed the room again. Close to thirty students waited with their heads upright, in earnest attention. Some politely folded their hands on their desk, while others sat ready with pen and notebook.

In a deliberate, slow manner, I conducted roll call, hoping a chunk of time passed with each name called. I promised myself not to look at the clock.

After attendance, I stepped from behind the lectern and leaned against the desk.

"Last Monday Mr. Striplen went over the syllabus, covering your reading assignments, class projects, and term papers. We didn't get a chance to know you as individuals, however. So let's take this opportunity to get to know each other. I'll start."

"My name is Pete Cruz . . ."

As I spoke, students showed favorable facial expressions when I hit upon each point about myself.

"Here's what we're looking for: your name, where you're from, your major—it's okay if you're undeclared—what you do in your spare time, what you'd like to get out of this class, and what you hope to do after you graduate. Who'd like to go next?"

Fear lessened its hold. They didn't know I had been assigned to fly solo only twenty minutes earlier.

So it went for the remainder of class. Time had burdened me before the start of class, but now it passed at a brisk pace, and I moved each introduction along so that all the students received a turn.

"Thank you, everyone," I said. "It was nice to meet you. Have a good next couple of days. We'll see you Friday."

Conducting the class by myself not only bolstered my confidence, but I discovered it to be both fun and rewarding.

The rest of my senior year flew by. My roommate, Ken, and I were involved with Circle K, a campus community service organization, and I was vice president of a fledgling club, the Filipino Student Association. I carried a full load of classes to assure I'd graduate on time, and I continued my part-time job as an EOP peer advisor.

My past as an uninvolved, insecure loner had turned an about-face. I knew so many people around campus that it seemed I stopped every fifty feet to talk to friends or acquaintances. What a far cry from grade school where I was an outsider and felt invisible!

As the spring 1980 semester ended, Ken and I hosted a large and raucous graduation party at a nearby neighborhood recreation center.

Mortar boards spun through the air like ninja throwing stars.

Standing in the midst of Hornet Field at Sac State, I posed for pictures with friends whom I probably wouldn't see again.

Scoop and Mimi were the only family who showed for my commencement. Cookie, Penny, and Buster lived out-of-state. I searched the stands for Mom, but never saw her. Pat later admitted he hadn't brought her because of his grudge against Scoop, even if it meant Mom missing my graduation ceremony. Although Mom wouldn't have said much, I was disappointed she wasn't there. Dad's absence from any of my activities was a given. If he had been there, I'd have been uncomfortable. But at the same time, it would have gone a long way to show that he cared.

Graduation produced a sober reminder that my life, for the time being, had reverted to my old normal.

31

My Way in San Jose

Two weeks after graduation, I returned to San Jose. Through Maxi's Bay Area contacts, I obtained a position with the Filipino Service Center of the Greater Santa Clara Valley and Vicinity (FSC). As the program coordinator, I administered a one-year federal contract to provide employment and referral services to newly arrived and low-income immigrants.

The staff consisted of an office assistant, three community service specialists, and two volunteers. The position came with my own office and free parking underneath the building.

My responsibilities included community outreach and attendance at the chamber of commerce and other civic meetings to promote our services. In addition, I connected with Filipino businesses in economically depressed areas of east San Jose, where many prospective clients lived.

The afternoon sun greeted me as I exited a small Filipino market. My day brightened with a successful sale of advertisement space in our agency newsletter. I paused on the dingy sidewalk to locate my car when the sound of someone walking in flip-flops came toward me. An older Filipina came into view.

"Hello," I said, smiling.

Kumusta. Magandang hapon. She greeted me in Tagalog.

"I don't speak the language."

Ikaw Filipino? Her words again escaped me, but she followed in English. "Are you Filipino?"

"Yes."

"You were born here?"

"Yes, here in San Jose." I lifted my shoulders with pride.

"Then you're not really a Filipino." Unsmiling, her eyes narrowed.

My throat constricted as if my tie were choking me.

"I got nothin' to say about that." My jaw tightened to contain my rising anger. Her comment implied I had sold out my heritage.

Eager to ditch a situation before I said something I might later regret, I stepped off the sidewalk without looking back.

On the drive to my office, I recollected other similar experiences.

During another time, I had explained to a Filipina that I spoke only English.

"You ought to be ashamed of yourself," she said. Shame burned inside of me when she uttered that reply. At the same time, I was bewildered because it wasn't my fault I didn't speak another language. I believed my parents chose to speak only English to their children because they encountered racism and discrimination. They wanted to give us the best chance for success by assimilating us into American culture.

The unfairness smoldered in my gut. It wasn't enough that I wore a shirt and tie and directed a non-profit agency whose services aided the Filipino community.

Shunned within my own culture—I was an outsider.

After several months, FSC hit benchmarks for job placement, social service referrals to other agencies, and numbers of clients served. We were on track for successful contract completion, which would usher an unhampered extension for the following year. I considered myself a first-rate administrator and supervisor.

After a morning break, I entered the employees' office and gave them orders before turning to go back to my office.

"Can I talk to you?" Annabelle, one of the community service specialists asked.

"Sure."

She looked me in the eye. Then her eyes darted to the other employees and back to me. When I glanced at them, they immediately hunched over their desks, pretending to be busy.

"In your office."

Annabelle seemed to be the appointed spokesperson.

Just past my doorway, she started.

"You have to stop treating us badly."

"What do you mean?"

"You order us around. You're not satisfied with anything we do. You never say anything good about our work. One of the volunteers said you yelled at her." Her complaints blurted out so fast I suspected she had practiced them beforehand.

"I, um." I said, and stopped. I didn't know what to say. I probed my mind for instances of bad behavior.

"You're a really nice guy, and I know this isn't like you. But we're doing the best we can."

I regretted losing my temper with the volunteer and wasn't surprised that the news got around. She was retired and unmotivated by working for free. It seemed she only wanted a place to pass the time. I had grown frustrated because I couldn't depend on her.

After thinking about it, I admitted to myself that I hadn't offered encouraging words or praise to anyone. Staff meetings were rare and unneeded in my view. My management method had been to issue directives on the fly and expect immediate follow-through without question.

"I'm sorry," I said. "I didn't realize how I was treating everybody. Thank you for bringing this to my attention."

Annabelle departed and I sat at my desk staring at the wall. I wondered if attaining successful federal grant statistics was worth the low staff morale. Could I be a kinder supervisor and still reach our goals?

Dad had said I'd never amount to anything. My biggest fear was that he could be right.

At lunch time, I plodded along the street in front of my building, my steps heavy with the realization that my childhood experiences had infected the workplace.

My own inescapable truth became clear—that no matter how hard I tried, it was never good enough. I was stuck in my past. How I performed at work and how I led the staff proved it. While growing up, I had never received compliments, support, or encouragement, so I never gave those things to others. My reward for perfection was that I wouldn't get yelled at.

The realization then hit me—I ran the FSC the same as Dad would have. He had become my model. I couldn't understand how I'd let that happen.

Another month passed at the FSC, but my heart was no longer in it. I couldn't get over thinking I had behaved just like Dad. I backed off from my heavy-handed management style. Though I was nicer to staff, my past behavior, coupled with my own guilt and paranoia, seemed to have created a general air of distrust and disunity.

In addition to my inability to work well with people, I harbored an increasing frustration and anger at myself for not seeing it or being able to do anything about it.

Back in hometown Milpitas, I was in familiar but uncertain territory. There were a few friends from high school with whom I hung out, but I withdrew into myself as I had throughout my growing years.

I fulfilled my one-year contract, and I made plans to return to Sacramento. I longed to return to where I had come of age and matured—the place that to me held the promise of a better life.

32

Back to Sac

I returned to Sacramento and rented a downtown studio apartment across from Mercy General Hospital. I was glad to be back, and I renewed acquaintances with many college friends who'd remained in the area.

My job at the Sacramento Medical Foundation Blood Bank provided a stepping-stone to life back in Sacramento. The pay was decent and the staff was fun. However, I didn't want to make it my career because there were few opportunities for promotion, and I disliked having to rotate through swing, graveyard, and weekend shifts.

In my spare time, I wanted to better myself, so I took meditation and yoga classes. I also enrolled in community adult-education workshops in topics related to self-actualization.

As I did while growing up, I found refuge in reading. I frequented bookstores' self-help sections. The gray cover of *Your Erroneous Zones* prompted me to appraise myself. An illustration showed words printed inside colored sections of an individual's silhouette, such as "Self-Rejection" in green, "Anger" and "Living in the Past" in red, and "Fear of the Unknown" in orange.

As if they were Cheetos Puffs, I devoured self-help books. To my stockpile, I added titles like *I'm OK—You're OK, The Road Less Traveled, Psycho-Cybernetics, Feel the Fear and Do It Anyway,* and *The Power of Positive Thinking.*

I studied each book, hoping to unlock the door to my prison of self-doubt, insecurity, lack of confidence, inadequacy, low self-esteem, and poor self-identity.

Despite my self-improvement efforts, an undercurrent of unease dogged me. The erroneous zone descriptions fit me well.

Eventually, I desired knowledge beyond what self-help books or workshops offered. I quit my job at the blood bank and returned to Sac State, where I enrolled in the master's in counseling program, a two-year undertaking to obtain a Marriage and Family Counseling Credential (MFCC).

I hoped to help myself and then assist others who had experienced similar life problems.

My first year as a graduate student went well. I achieved superior grades and learned a lot about myself and the effects of a dysfunctional upbringing.

In the summer, I landed a job as a youth counselor for Asian Resources, Inc., a public non-profit agency in South Sacramento.

In my third semester of grad school, I planned to continue the second half of the program.

"This is what we're going to do," Professor Parson said as he looked around the room. "Remain standing, and when you're ready, go stand next to the person whom you believe you most closely relate to. It's okay if there's more than two in a group."

Anxiety tweaked my innards. Despite my self-taught social skills, I still considered myself a loner who didn't fit in.

The classroom seemed to shrink to the size of a child's playhouse. Through the narrow, vertical windows, the sun had set to darkness.

As I looked around the room, I doubted I closely related to anyone. I searched for classmates with whom I had something in common.

Other than the professor, I was the only guy in the room. I guessed most men were in business or engineering courses.

In hindsight, I should've stood next to the professor, but even then, I regarded male teachers as Dad-like authority figures.

So I scanned the room for skin tone or eye shapes similar to mine. I appeared to be the only person of color. I related to no one.

There were times during my youth when captains chose sides for teams. Before anyone knew of my athletic prowess, I was the smallish, slight boy who got picked last. My position: left out.

I felt like that skinny, overlooked boy now.

Shuffling feet snapped me out of contemplation. Murmurs and stifled laughter joined in as students began to meet each other.

Too late to leave. I had nowhere to go. In grade school, I found a fence to lean against or a bench to sit on by myself. Not so now.

My vulnerability was draped on full display. A mental sign hung from my neck: "I don't belong anywhere."

I feared Professor Parson would downgrade me for not following directions or being uncooperative. I imagined myself on a raft, adrift without oars.

Shuffling feet slowed to a stop and small talk halted as participants found their kindred classmates.

A sheen of perspiration broke across my forehead. I continued to look about as desperation overtook me.

The entire class seemed to be watching, waiting to see if I related to anyone. Did I see pity in their eyes?

I looked past groups of twos and threes and toward the back, until I saw someone alone. She remained at her desk listening with her hands clasped in front of her. She was blond, slender, young, and blind.

As I made my way toward her, classmates parted as if I were a leper. Perhaps they hoped I wasn't coming to join them.

Sarah, the sightless student, turned her head to the side to listen as I approached. I didn't say anything because I was trying to compose myself.

Relief seemed to settle on her, perhaps after she heard my shallow breaths. Did she also wonder if she belonged anywhere? She seemed curious, certainly wondering who stood next to her. I remained quiet, thankful I'd found someone to stand next to.

Professor Parson began the lesson. He talked about how we relate to others on conscious and subconscious levels. At the exercise's conclusion, he nodded at me as we broke to return to our desks. I wondered if he meant to acknowledge my difficulty.

"Thank you," I said to Sarah.

"Bye," she answered. Her smile seemed to suggest thankfulness.

I picked Sarah because I spent my growing years feeling alone. I imagined that due to her affliction, she may have been like me—viewed as someone different and with few friends.

Although her blindness may have limited her, I believed my upbringing had disabled me—an outsider in my own family, unable to join sports teams, not having many friends through grade school, and excluded by my own culture because I was too Americanized.

Through the entire semester, each class reminded me I wasn't like anyone else, and my psychological barriers prevented me from joining or becoming part of any group.

At the end of the semester, I withdrew from the master's in counseling program, having forty-five of sixty units completed.

Years later, I wondered if I had reacted on a subconscious level to Dad's insistence that I couldn't do anything right and would never amount to anything. I feared success because any accomplishments I had while growing up weren't celebrated. I feared failure because it would make Dad prophetic and lower my already low self-esteem. I feared commitment because it confronted me with my fear of success or failure.

Like Sarah, I was blind to seeing that I belonged anywhere.

A rare photo of Dad, circa 1940.

The author in his mother's arms.
With his family in Milpitas, CA, circa 1958.

Top Row: Cookie, Pat, Penny.
Bottom: Peewee, Buster, Scoop, Mom
San Jose, CA, circa 1959.

Pat, Peewee, Scoop, Buster
San Jose, CA, circa 1961.

2016—At a Sacramento Kings basketball game with Natalia.

2022—Natalia graduates with a master's degree
from Biola University.

33

Sole Searching

In a feeble attempt to hold off match point, my ball rebounded off the net and dribbled back toward me. "Dang it! How could I do that? I'm just a freakin' moron!" I shrieked skyward, wagged my tongue, shook my head, and high-stepped in place like a maniacal Mick Jagger.

My tantrum escalated as I flung my racket. It spun like a whirlybird, bounced off the net, and clattered to the court.

I hated to lose, but I especially suffered when I gave the win away by my own error.

Clutching my hips, I walked a slow circle, staring at the asphalt and fuming about how I blew the simplest of shots.

Robert, a regular tennis partner, waited at the net to shake hands after our *friendly* match.

"Nice game," I said, extending my hand. "I'm sorry for losing my temper. I can't believe I missed that last shot. It sat up just right. All I needed to do was tap it over."

"That's okay," Robert said in a calm, even tone. "I understand. I don't like to lose either."

We gathered our gear and then walked from the court in McKinley Park in midtown Sacramento.

"My feet hurt," I said. "Don't yours?" Our match lasted more than an hour, and as usual I played all out.

"No," Robert answered after glancing at me. We walked to our cars and planned our next match.

After he drove away, I sat in my car and wondered, *Why do my feet hurt and his don't?*

"Describe how it feels," Dr. Stevens, the podiatrist, said. His folded arms and serious expression conveyed an expectation for accuracy that I couldn't deliver.

I returned his gaze with my own baffled look.

"Is it sharp? Some people describe it as walking with a pebble in their shoe."

"I can't say it's sharp. Although sometimes when I take a step there's a jolt."

"Others say it's like walking on hot coals," the doctor continued.

"It's on the soles of both of my feet. The best I can say is it's like when you sit for a long time on aluminum bleachers at a football game. After a while, your butt hurts and you have to stand. My feet are like when my butt hurts."

A light bulb didn't switch on in his face. He didn't indicate that he knew what unfailing remedy to prescribe.

"Are your heels tight when you get out of bed?" I realized foot care is an inexact science. He relied on his own opinion. My confidence in him faltered.

"Yeah, I guess. I'm not sure I notice."

"I believe you have plantar fasciitis. Some athletes get this, and someone like you who is very active is prone to it."

Why couldn't I be one of those who didn't get it? Plantar-whatever appeared to be his go-to, catch-all diagnosis.

"With your permission, here's what I'd like to do," he said. "An injection of cortisone usually takes care of it. It'll shrink the inflammation." He exited the room, leaving me to my anxiety.

I had envisioned a brief appointment where I'd be told to wear different shoes or use an ointment. I didn't like the "usually takes care of it" part. It left too much room for the un-usual.

Dr. Stevens returned and walked to a cabinet area where he stood with his back to me. Small instruments clinked on a chrome tray.

He twirled to face me, reminding me of a magician ready for his next trick. Instead of a wand, he grasped a long needle resembling an ice pick. I wished I could do a disappearing act.

Dr. Stevens sprayed an ice spray on the side of my heel. A deep cold sensation overwhelmed the targeted area as he pushed the needle into my foot. I emitted an audible gasp at the sight of half of the needle disappearing into my foot. He wiggled the needle around and pumped cortisone into my heel.

"The area will feel numb for a few hours. You can apply regular pressure to it and walk normally."

Feeling as if my foot were encased in Styrofoam, I limped out the door.

Later in the day, I took tentative steps, but couldn't tell if the medical procedure succeeded.

Pain returned the next day.

In the ensuing months, I followed a regimen of stretching exercises, creams, icing, strapping, and nonsteroidal anti-inflammatory drugs.

Nothing worked. Relief came only when I stayed off my feet.

From my parked car, I stared wistfully at the tennis courts.

It'd been half a year since I last played, but I couldn't play anymore because of pain in both feet.

In the past, I headed to the tennis courts after work. Job concerns dissolved when my only focus was on the ball and pounding it with my racket.

I tried swimming and bicycling, but they weren't the same.

Gone was my lifestyle, my passion, my self-identity, my primary means of releasing stress.

A tear fell from the corner of my eye.

Pain had changed my life. Grocery shopping on one day meant I couldn't work in the yard until the next day or two. I didn't have many friends because I was reluctant to go anywhere. After too much time on my feet, I needed to lie down. Pain sapped my energy. Sometimes all I could do was sit.

Numerous medical disciplines could not determine its cause. Over the years, it never healed but gradually became worse. I looked like a normal, healthy human being. Yet whenever I was on my feet, I experienced pain.

Somewhat like growing up, no one knew of the abuse I endured at home.

34

A Successful Interview

The Asian Resources, Summer Youth Employment & Training Program (SYETP) was a whirlwind of activity. From day one, it involved screening as many as 400 applicants for more than 150 subsidized summer jobs.

After serving as a youth employment counselor the previous year, I was promoted to program director for the summer. Hiring two clerical staff and four counselors was my immediate need.

During the day's interview schedule, a cancellation resulted in a welcome break. I dawdled in the reception area, waiting for the next interviewee to arrive.

I reclined in an office chair surrounded by wood-paneled walls that twenty years earlier had been chic.

"How are the interviews going?" Linda, the office manager, came in. Her eyes were wide open and expressive. "Find any good ones?"

"Oh, yeah. Clerical staff was easy. We're okay there. But for the youth counselors, it's hard to tell if they'd be good working with kids." I contemplated the need for good counselors to ensure a successful program. "Who's up next on the schedule?"

"At three o'clock, there's Martina Rico."

I vaguely remembered the names. After two days of interviews, they all blended together.

At 2:50 p.m. I observed a woman park, exit her car, and come toward the entrance. She wore an at-the-knee beige skirt, a white blouse, and a long, thin, light-pink sweater that ended at her hips. Her professional attire gave her away as our next interviewee. As she approached, she appeared to be Latina, with smooth and unblemished bronze skin. Her shoulder-length hair had a wavy black sheen.

She walked with a purposeful gait.

I sat transfixed.

"Pete, stick your eyes back inside your head!" Linda cried. "You don't want them bulging out when she comes in." She grinned and awaited my usual comeback.

"She's hired," I said, feigning seriousness.

"You better not go there. I know you." Linda's chortles filled the room.

"That's why we have a panel—to compensate for any biases on my part."

Linda exited to greet her at the front door, and I bent an ear to their muffled voices. Linda entered with her, and in one swift motion I swept back my hair, adjusted my tie, and rose from my chair.

"Pete, this is Martina Rico," Linda said. "She's here to interview for one of the youth counselor positions."

"Nice to meet you, Martina," I said. She looked at me wide-eyed with a warm smile. Up close she was even more attractive. I drew in my breath and extended my hand. Her perfume carried a scent of strawberries. "Thank you for coming."

When I realized I hadn't let go of her hand, I stopped speaking. I released my grip and folded my hands to hide my embarrassment.

"I'll inform the panel you've arrived. Be right back."

———

Martina made the cut for one of the youth counselor positions based on her experience, her current enrollment in the master's in social work program at Sac State, and her fluency in speaking and writing Spanish.

The youth counselors occupied a separate room. Each of their desks was placed at one of the corners. On occasion, I strolled into their office to ask about a particular participant or placement.

Because of the job's temporary nature, counselors rarely decorated their work areas with anything beyond their own coffee cups. At one point, I noticed a calendar on Martina's wall. It pictured a well-dressed Asian guy who could've come from the pages of *GQ* magazine. I said nothing and left.

The SYETP kept me too preoccupied to think about anything other than its operations.

———

At home I poured beer from a bottle into a glass and welcomed the end of another week of nonstop activity. I was determined to conclude the final weeks of the SYETP program on a strong note.

While settled in my easy chair, I considered the night's TV fare. The phone rang.

"Hello?"

"Hello, Pete?"

"Yes, this is Pete. Who's this?"

"This is Martina from work."

During employee orientation, I had furnished my home telephone number to the staff and invited them to call me for any reason. I assumed Martina had left something in the office, wanted to request time off, or called on behalf of her coworkers to complain about my dictatorial ways. "Hi, Martina. How's it going?"

"Fine. Umm, I want to know if you'd like to come over for dinner."

Ah, nothing serious.

"Is this a potluck with everyone? What should I bring?"

"Oh no, it's just me calling. I'm asking only you."

"Oh, okay. I'm sorry. I get it. When?"

"Tomorrow, if you're free."

"We could do that. The program ends in a few weeks, so I don't think there's a conflict of interest." I chuckled. "Regardless, you're still going to get a good evaluation."

"No, I'm not thinking that. I just wanted to get to know you."

"I'm a bit surprised. You don't think I'm too demanding?"

"You are, but you're more demanding of yourself than anyone else. We talk in the office about how we don't want to get swept up by the fast pace of the program."

"Yeah, I try not to let others get too caught up in it either. After all, it's just a summer job for you guys."

"Behind all that, you seem to be a really nice guy."

"Thanks. I like to think I am." I recollected the times I'd seen Martina in the course of work. Her calendar, picturing different Asian guys for each month, came to mind. "Does this have anything to do with the calendar on your office wall? Because if it does, I'm nothing like those dudes. I suppose I could slick my hair back with a little pomade and get myself a tailor-made suit."

"That was for your benefit," Martina said. "I wanted you to see that I liked Asian men."

"I'm clueless. The summer program moves so fast I barely have time to think."

"I thought there might be something between us the first time we met."

I recalled my lingering handshake when Linda introduced us—and how I had gazed at her as she walked in from the parking lot.

Martina's candid interest was refreshing.

"Should I bring anything?"

"No, just yourself."

I liked hearing I was good enough.

After the summer program concluded, Asian Resources, SYETP, received a 96 percent rating.

The real prize? Martina and I began a courtship that ended in marriage three years later.

Our dating life activities were spent enjoying breakfast at quaint coffee shops, day trips to the Monterey coast, and Sac State basketball and football games. It was an idyllic life that was like taking a nice offshore swim, but not knowing of the dangerous undertow.

35

Married Strife

"**D**on't talk to me like that! You don't know what you're talking about!" "Leave me alone!" resounded through our home. Not more than a week after Martina and I had returned from our honeymoon, that old, ugly fear in me rose up. In addition to yelling, I hurled objects across the room and punched holes in walls and doors.

Martina had become my family. Therefore, I now viewed her as a threat. What before were mild observations, I now perceived as harsh criticisms and judgments. Her questions became accusations and interrogations. Nothing I or she did was good enough. Fear turned to anger and combusted into a blazing fire.

My ferocious behavior came from desperation to protect the defenseless, helpless child within me.

Martina and I had begun our married life in a cozy, small 1950s house with early California charm. It had white painted wood siding, a modest porch, and a huge shade tree that kept us cool during summer months.

As a new husband, I had difficulty finding my way, and our relationship darkened.

I worked a one-year contract as a consultant to the State Department of Rehabilitation, where I assessed injured or disabled clients' transferable skills and conducted weekly job search workshops. Martina worked part-time and continued studying for a master's degree in counseling.

In both private and public, I smoldered and erupted. I glowered at people; my eyes felt like twin blast furnaces. The chip on my shoulder seemed apparent from yards away. I gritted my teeth and grimaced like my boyhood idol, Batman, a dark crusader who sought to crush every wrong, to adjust the unjust.

One time I said to Martina, "I'm going to talk to that guy." She knew it was my euphemism to get in the face of an unsuspecting man who looked at me the wrong way.

"No! No!" Martina implored. She stood firm in front of me, pushing me back with two hands. "Leave him alone."

I went up to him anyway.

"Look, I don't want to fight you," he said.

Despite my short stature, every confrontation resulted in their surrender because there was no backing down in me.

Despite my failings, Martina and I forged ahead in our marriage. Sometimes she tried to make me aware of my off-putting remarks. "That sounds like a put-down," or "That hurts," she said.

When she gently said, "You had an episode," I had only been a heartbeat away from blowing up at her.

My rage became like my father's. I interpreted every encounter as a criticism of who I was. I took everything personally, and I righteously defended myself. After each incident, I felt guilt over my behavior. I felt ashamed and believed my conduct was worse than his.

Eventually, our married life settled into a routine. Martina became a social worker for Sacramento County. On most weekends, she visited her family, where she obtained stability, love, and support—qualities absent in our household.

I visited her family only on certain occasions. For the most part, getting together with any family was awkward to me. I usually felt as uncomfortable as I had with my own family. Despite my in-law's efforts to make me feel at home, I normally felt uneasy and restless.

When my consultant contract expired, I didn't renew it. I obtained a permanent full-time position with the State of California. Civil service employment provided long-term security and benefits, which I couldn't get in private, non-profit agencies or in self-employment.

Married Strife

———

Until I was married, I had never had a birthday party. Martina provided a surprise party and tried to recapture the birthday celebrations I had missed. One year she decorated the kitchen and the cake with a Batman theme.

Though I'll always be grateful to her for trying, I couldn't relive something that never was. I thanked her and pretended to enjoy myself. Instead, it became a reminder of all the birthday celebrations I'd never had. Present time couldn't make up for the past. The empty well of missed acknowledgments couldn't be filled.

Martina's family members phoned me with well-wishes, as was her family's tradition. When they called, I felt significant and valued. My birthday meant something to someone.

My own family greetings were sporadic. In a good year, I received a card from Mimi and maybe one other sibling. Although I didn't send many birthday cards to my family either, I wondered what I'd done to cause those who didn't send me one to dislike me.

I wrote a letter to Dad to express my thoughts and feelings about his negative impact on my life, but I never sent it. I didn't want to deal with the fear and anxiety of wondering about his reactions. I believed he'd either not respond, or I'd receive a scathing reply in writing, over the phone, or the next time I visited him.

It was at least cathartic to write out my feelings.

36

Darkness Descending

"Hey, mijo" ("mijo" is a Spanish word that literally means "my son" but is also a term of endearment).

I hadn't realized I brushed past my lead person, Maria, on my way to the conference room.

Maria, a heavyset Latina with short, wavy hair and black-framed glasses, had taken me under her wing, making sure I had my work needs met.

"You okay?" she said with concern in her face. "You look sad today."

"Yeah, sorry. I'm all right. I was thinking about my dog."

"Really? What happened?"

"He died."

"Oh, I'm so sorry. We can be so close to our pets. What was his name?"

"Ebony."

Twenty years earlier, Dad had stolen him from my life. I didn't tell Maria that part.

Perhaps the stressful work environment reminded me of my upbringing, but something triggered my thoughts about the loss of my dog.

Did Ebony die on the day he disappeared? Dad wasn't the kind of person to take the trouble to drop off Ebony at the dog pound. Did he kill him and then bury him in the backyard? Did he throw my dog in the garbage can?

Alone in our conference room, I dabbed at the moisture stinging my eyes.

Decades after Ebony's death, I finally grieved.

The ribbon of highway stretched in front of me as my Harley-Davidson rumbled beneath me. I rounded each curve with confidence, weaving around cars like a downhill skier negotiating slaloms. Speed and the deep, vibrant sound of a powerful engine normally exhilarated me.

Yet just as I did while a teen, I wrestled with self-destructive thoughts. As I approached cars in anticipation of passing them, I deliberated whether to clip their back bumpers with my front wheel, which would throw me onto the pavement and to possible death. More than once, I considered falling from my bike in front of a close following vehicle so it would run over me.

Because I feared it wouldn't be successful and would just leave me worse off, I didn't follow through. I might get too mangled to lead an ordinary life, or incur heavy financial consequences, or live in a vegetative state of my own doing.

Instead, I envisioned copying the classic film, *Thelma and Louise*, where two women rocket off a cliff in their Ford Mustang. Like them, flying through the air and crashing my motorcycle would ensure certain death.

Despite my marriage to a wonderful woman who tolerated my many issues, I lived a joyless life. Because of chronic pain still in both feet, my physical and social activities remained few. And I had few friends.

Though I liked my fellow employees, I presented a casual, friendly facade throughout the day. In my cubicle, I sat alone with my thoughts.

An underlying bleakness clung to me like an unending fog.

I reached for the doorknob to the office of my primary care physician, Dr. Marasigan, but I retracted my hand as if it were too hot to touch. I did an about-face and fled around the corner. Martina followed, confused by my retreat.

"I can't go in."

"I'll talk to the receptionist." Martina left and I waited, stewing in fear and anxiety.

Led by Martina, Clare, one of my doctor's two receptionists, arrived. She pursed her lips and caution reflected in her eyes. I gathered she didn't know what to make of me. For more than five years, I'd been a regular patient, always greeted with a "Hi, Pete" or "Hello, Mr. Cruz" when I entered. I'd enjoyed the humorous exchanges between us during check-in.

Now, nothing was funny.

"What's going on, Pete? Your wife says you don't want to come in." Her lilting Filipino accent conveyed concern.

"I don't know. I couldn't go to work this morning. I guess I'm depressed."

My shoulders sagged and my head drooped as I stared aimlessly at the pavement. No aspirin could make my inner pain go away.

"Let me talk to Dr. Marasigan. I'll be right back."

Martina and I waited in silence. She reached to grasp my hand, but I withdrew it and folded my arms tight to my body, trying to keep myself together. A dark force surrounded me, siphoned my energy, withered my self-will, dissolved my spirit, and threatened to crush me.

Clare appeared again, her walk more purposeful. She held a square piece of paper that I recognized as being from Dr. Marasigan's prescription pad.

"I have a doctor's note excusing you from work for one week."

She produced another piece of paper and handed it to me. "You have an appointment to go here today." Written in pen was the name of a psychiatric hospital located on the outskirts of Sacramento.

"What time . . . is . . . my . . . appointment?" My words required effort, and I drawled like a drunken cowboy.

"They're waiting for you. I told them you'd be there by noon." Clare attempted a reassuring smile. She turned to Martina. "Bring some personal belongings for him—a toothbrush and some clothes. They might want him to stay."

"Okay, we'll do that," Martina nodded. Her eyes widened at the seriousness of the situation.

Clare turned back to me. "Dr. Marasigan wanted me to tell you that if you have any problems with your work or with your appointment at the hospital today, to let him know. He said he'd call them himself."

I'd usually held Dr. Marasigan at arm's length. He, like my father, was an older Filipino, but his mannerisms eased my fears. On one occasion, he patted the rounded pudge of my stomach. "What's that? Aren't you getting enough exercise?" He laughed, completely different from Dad's harsh criticisms and demands.

After hearing Clare's message from him, I reconsidered my feelings for him. He truly cared about me.

I desperately searched for more positive thoughts or feelings. The darkness of my life had begun to overpower me.

37

In Despair

"**P**ete, please come with me," said the nurse. She assured Martina I'd be well cared for, but to expect a call within the next hour to advise her on when she could pick me up.

I hugged Martina, but like most things lately, my embrace was weak and noncommittal.

"You'll be all right," she said. My wife clasped my hand and squeezed it while gazing in my eyes.

More than anyone else, Martina knew the troubled life I'd led. She was the only one who had seen my many frenzies and witnessed firsthand the demons I could not escape.

My steps were cumbersome, and I drooped in despair. The nurse walked alongside.

Except for the movie *One Flew Over the Cuckoo's Nest,* I had no concept of mental-health institutions. I imagined she'd hand me a paper cup filled with mind-numbing pills or I'd be rendered listless by electroshock therapy.

"I can see that you're depressed." The nurse turned toward me. "You have minimal eye contact. Your affect is flat." I didn't know what she meant, but I was sure the effect of depression had flattened me.

We settled into a small office where I filled out paperwork.

"Sometimes a person needs a break, that's all. This place is good for that," she gently said while reviewing my forms. "I see that you work. It looks like you've been employed in good jobs and stayed there. You've graduated college. You probably don't belong in a place like this."

If I didn't belong, what was I doing there? I couldn't grasp what she meant.

"For now, you're on seventy-two-hour hold, which means you're bound by law to stay with us while we assess whether you're a harm to yourself or others. You'll see your doctor later today."

The room I shared with another person was narrow and windowless. The beds were parallel against the walls to each other and had small nightstands with space enough for personal items. My roommate lay motionless and soundless on his bed. With his pillow over his head, all I saw were random strands of long, sandy hair.

With my hands clasped behind my head, I lay on my back to stare at the ceiling and ponder my fate. I had nowhere to go and nowhere to be.

Depression seemed like suspended animation, frozen in mind and body.

I felt disconnected from physical sensations and unmoved by thoughts or desires.

"Pete?" I glanced at the young man in the doorway. He smiled. He wore white pants and a white polo shirt, form-fitted to his husky torso.

I nodded.

"I'm here to take you to your doctor's office. You ready?"

"Okay." I sat up on my bed, slipped on my shoes, and rose in slow motion to gain my bearings.

He guided me along corridors and through several secured accessways. We stopped at a door where a brass plate inscribed with "Stewart Jarvis, MD" faced me at eye level.

The orderly knocked twice and opened the door. "Pete Cruz," he spoke into the room.

"Yes," Dr. Jarvis answered. "Come in."

After the door shut behind me, the doctor motioned me to a chair in front of his expansive cherrywood desk and said nothing. He scrutinized me as if he were sitting behind a judge's bench.

While he reviewed my file, I peered at his plaques and diplomas, which displayed his medical and psychiatric degrees, as well as his professional honors and associations. Many, with ornate frames, seemed oversized. Maybe he resented the term *shrink* attached to his profession.

Since he hadn't greeted me, and despite his professional pedigree, I didn't believe he'd earned the right to order me to sit with a sweep of his hand as a king would his subject.

His thinning hair receded, accentuating a broad forehead, which wrinkled while he examined my file. His three-piece suit and silk tie added to a picture of self-importance.

"You're to begin an antidepressant immediately, without question," he said abruptly from his throne.

Besides the unasked, *Who do you think you are?* I had no questions.

"I will prescribe you Prozac." He enunciated his words with a gravelly voice and contorted his face for emphasis. "If you decline, then there is no way I will allow your discharge from this hospital at the end of seventy-two hours." His arms skirted across his desk as if he were reciting a Shakespearean tragedy.

"I got it," I said. My facial expression remained blank, giving him little to read, as I'd always done with Dad.

"I spoke with your supervisor, Sherry, today," Martina said during visiting hours. I began to feel guilty about missing work and believed I had let Sherry down. I was certain my vaunted work ethic had sustained major damage. "She's a very nice person and cares about you. She says her brother has depression and to take all the time you need."

The wrenching turns within my stomach eased. I was glad my supervisor understood what I was going through. I promised myself to make it up to Sherry when I returned.

"I called a few other people to let them know you were here. But no one in your family."

"Thanks." I shrugged, unable to express outward emotion or ask who else she'd told.

I was grateful because I didn't want family, especially Dad, to know how far I'd fallen.

Shame and humiliation covered me like an umbrella, then collapsed and closed to drench me in cold raindrops of despair.

38

What They Missed

The next day after breakfast, I wandered to the recreation area. When I arrived, most inpatients kept to themselves. Some glanced at me, but went back to avoiding eye contact. Board games lay unused on a table. A game show blared on the TV.

I read in my room for a while and then roamed to allowed areas. I moved slowly like a vacuum cleaner robot.

In the afternoon, I again lay in bed and stared at the ceiling. My mysterious, pillow-covered roommate had disappeared. His bed was made and the nightstand was empty. I speculated he probably had been assigned to another room with padded walls.

"Group therapy in fifteen minutes, conference room." That familiar phrase from the day before was repeated down the hallway.

The messenger's head popped into my doorway, then vanished after repeating the announcement. I was eager to go, convinced that isolation and boredom was the hospital's intentional plan to motivate patients to be active.

Carefully closing the door behind me, I stepped inside. I looked for someone in authority at the table. That person sat with a clipboard in front of him. He smiled slightly and motioned to an open seat. His curly hair looked like bedsprings gone awry, but underscored by nerdy wire-rimmed glasses.

Except for the counselor, females made up the group.

A few glanced at me, but most seemed caught up within themselves. No one spoke a word. Some appeared somber, staring ahead, while others looked down at their laps.

I'd never been with a group of dejected and despondent women, and I restrained an urge to blurt out, "What happened? Miss the sale at Macy's?" But I thought better of it, choosing not to be fitted in the latest fashion of men's straightjacket outerwear.

The group therapy counselor stood to provide instructions. He dispensed information without asking us to introduce ourselves, probably thinking no one cared to remember.

"Let's go around," he said. "I'd like each of you to answer: What do you miss?"

Chairs creaked when some women squirmed. Other women peered downward or to the side, perhaps to gather their thoughts or sift through reminders of painful experiences.

The counselor turned to the participant closest to him.

"I miss my dad," she answered with a cheerless expression.

"I miss my dad." The next person gave the same answer. She stifled a sob and mentioned something about his untimely death when she was a teenager.

I miss my dad caused a chain reaction of identical answers, one woman after another. With the exception of one or two different responses, dads were overwhelmingly missing in action. *Family Feud* host Steve Harvey could've announced, "We surveyed one hundred people from our studio audience for an answer to this question: What do you miss?" A narrow card flipped to its other side as he yelled, "Survey says: I miss my dad."

I was 100 percent certain my dad would be the last thing I missed. The only way I could miss my dad was if I'd launched a stink bomb at him and it fell off target.

"I miss playing tennis and basketball," I said. I mentioned my chronic foot pain, but didn't elaborate to this group that expressed zero reaction.

While the counselor talked about grief and regret, I pondered the powerful influence of a dad in a daughter's life. The pain of their losses left a lasting impression.

39

Valued Visitors

A**l Striplen sat** in the visiting area, where I'd been summoned after dinner. I had been his teaching assistant at Sac State, and he became my assigned counselor after Satsuki left to pursue her doctorate.

After I graduated, we often met and he became my friend and mentor. I was surprised to see him.

"Thanks for coming, Al. I guess my wife called you?" Embarrassment settled on my shoulders.

He smiled his same pleasant, accepting smile. Meeting him at a psychiatric hospital seemed no different than sitting with him at a coffee shop.

"You know, I had planned to go camping, but then some things came up and I couldn't go. The next day, something else came up. I had to tell myself, 'I'm not supposed to go.' Then Martina called and I knew why."

We discussed my troubled, stagnant life that had descended into depression.

"This is just a blip in your life, a temporary setback," Al said, as if it were my destiny to be free of misery.

A future unburdened by despair was hard to envision.

"A guy like you doesn't stay hidden," he said. "The cream always rises to the top." I'd never pictured myself as cream rising. Depression kept a lid on it.

At the close of visiting hours, we hugged and made plans to get together after my release.

The final day of my seventy-two-hour hold was uneventful. I played ping-pong with another inpatient, read magazines, and wrote in a journal.

In the afternoon, I met with Dr. Jarvis to discuss the effects of the medication. He authorized my release for the next day.

In the early evening, after a brief visit from Martina, I returned to my room. Soon I was called back to meet another visitor.

There sat Satsuki, my original counselor when I was a Sac State freshman. She regarded me with a purposeful stare when I walked to her.

"I don't know why I'm surprised, but I'm glad you're here," I said. I hadn't kept in contact with her as I had with Al, but whenever I called, she always made time for me.

"You know I'll always be here for you," she said, smiling. I never felt judged when she looked at me. She had a not-a-wasted-moment energy about her, but I never felt rushed. In the past, she had coaxed me, "Pete, get off your ass and do something about it." She was the only person I knew who could utter an expletive and not mean it like a swear word. I suspected I might be due for another get-off-your-duff advisory.

We discussed my experiences in the hospital and my life struggles. I believed I had let her down, though I doubted she would think of it that way. But I'd always wanted to make her proud.

A single red rose lay on the table, but I didn't think anything of it. She picked it up.

"Look at this." The stem was as long as her arm, the petals tightly closed. "Look at this," she said again, and peered into my eyes. "This is you. It's beautiful. A single one is perfect."

She was right about one thing—the rose was perfect. But I wasn't.

"Think about what it takes to get to this point. It's come up from the dirt, the grime, the mud, and all the crap that it had to endure to get to this state. Yet as beautiful as it is now, it—like you—has yet to bloom."

Straightening up in my chair, I hung on her every word.

"It will be even more beautiful in its final state."

Her piercing eyes gazed at me, and I nodded for her to continue.

"But look, there are thorns. Thorns are a part of life. They stick you, point at you, and are even painful."

She taught masters-in-counseling classes at Sac State. No doubt her students were enthralled.

"Take this. I want you to have it." She handed me the rose. "Take it back to your room and think about who you are."

"Thank you, Satsuki," I stammered.

She grasped my hands in hers.

"Know this, Pete," she said, forcefully. "You are dear to me. I care very much about you."

"I know," I said. My lower lip trembled and my eyes teared, yet my belief system still fought against admitting someone cared.

She regarded me for a moment and seemed to gather her thoughts.

"I've been careful about taking you on as a client because we don't have that kind of relationship," she said. "Sometimes I think I'm like your mean aunt who wants to whip you into shape." She chuckled. "I'm willing to take you on as a client if it will help you."

"Yeah, I guess so. You know me." Gratitude filled my heart.

"Okay. Call my office to set up an appointment. Tell them I spoke with you and let them know I said it's okay for them to schedule you."

"Thanks for seeing me here, Satsuki. It means a lot to me."

"Anytime. Now give me a hug."

I stood and circled my arms around her.

"Thanks," I said, and stepped apart.

"No." She pulled me back. "Give me a real hug." She held me tightly.

I felt uncomfortable, not used to anyone holding me so long.

"Don't say anything. Breathe. Just be here," she said, perhaps sensing my urge to flee. "I'm not going to hurt you."

In time, she stepped back and looked at me.

"Okay?" she said. Her smile expressed reassurance.

"Okay," I said, smiling back.

I strolled back to my room with the rose in hand. A thorn pricked my finger, but the pain hardly registered.

What would my life have been like if I had had parents like Al and Satsuki?

The antidepressants seemed to have minimal effect on my outlook, and I was eventually eased off them. Instead, I had weekly counseling sessions with Satsuki for several months and settled into a normal life with Martina.

My home and work life had stabilized enough that I had something important to do—a search of the past.

40

Loved and Not Forgotten

Taking a community adult-education course, "Be Your Own Detective," opened my hopes to jump-start my search for my little brother, Perry. When we had moved from the farms in San Jose to a middle-class neighborhood in Milpitas, Perry didn't make the move with us.

"Becoming your own detective is a lot easier than you might think," the instructor said. "Tell me what you're looking for."

From my seat, front and center, my hand shot upward.

"I'm looking for a grave."

"I don't know," she said, cupping her chin with her thumb and index finger. "I've never been asked that question. I'm not sure where I would begin."

Did I waste an evening and a class fee?

"It's a state office downtown," someone in the back said. I turned and beheld a man perhaps ten years my senior. "You'll have to request a death certificate. It'll say where the cemetery's located."

"Thank you," I smiled.

"There's a form you'll need," he continued. "Wait. I happen to have one with me."

Who would have thought?

"Here it is." He passed it up to me. "You can have that. They'll ask for an eight-dollar fee."

I would've paid hundreds.

"Application for Certified Copy of Death Record" lay in my hands. I couldn't believe it. I'd grown up in a godless household. Now in my late thirties, receiving this vital information seemed too coincidental. *Maybe there is a God who actually cares about me.*

Recollections of my little brother, Perry, were fleeting. We had rolled around on the floor as kids. He followed me outside to look at stuff on our San Jose farmland.

He was three and I was seven at the time of his passing. There was no funeral. Not a word was spoken about him. No photos remained.

Over the years, I had asked Mom, "Where's Perry buried?"

"I don't know," she said. I didn't believe her. Maybe the loss of a son pushed her into denial, but I couldn't forget my little brother, Perry.

———

More than thirty years after his death, I found his burial grounds.

The memorial park's office at the Santa Clara Mission Catholic Cemetery was a small, nondescript building. Inside, a man not much older than I stood behind a counter.

"Hi. My name's Mike. How can I help you?"

"I'm looking for my brother's grave. His name is Perry Cruz."

"Sure. Let me take a look." Mike furrowed his brow. "I'm not seeing it. You're sure he's here?"

"Yes, he was just a baby. He died about thirty years ago. Here's his death record."

He examined my document.

"Oh. I'll need to look in our archives." He did a one-eighty and entered a room the size of a walk-in closet. Large rolled-up documents lay inside compartments like bottles in a wine rack. He extracted one.

He unrolled the document on the counter and pointed. "Here he is. Block 21-X." The block comprised two vertical rows of boxes where someone with skillful penmanship had printed numerous last names. "We can go out there now."

My heart warmed at the thought.

"Let's take the cart." The burial grounds were extensive.

On the ride over, Mike didn't say much. For someone I'd perceived as outgoing, he seemed pensive. After we stopped, Mike took a few steps and looked about.

"It's right here."

"What?"

"Here." He tapped his foot on the roadway.

"Here?" I repeated, and pointed past the hedges to the rows of graves.

Mike, my guide, seemed downcast, perhaps his normal behavior when ushering grieving clients.

"No, right here. It's been paved over."

"You mean under?" I tapped the asphalt with my foot. My voice wavered. "He's under here?"

"It was a county burial," Mike said. He unfolded a small copy of the block map. "He's in row ten, about where we're standing."

"Why is there a road here?"

"I was just a kid myself, following my dad around." He waved his open hand to the direction of the office. "We were expanding out there and needed additional access. No one has ever come looking for someone in this block. Until now."

"No headstones?" My throat clinched as I came to grips that my brother's grave wasn't anything I could see or touch.

"The county buries the deceased when the parents can't afford it. In most cases, they're stillborn."

Perry was more than three years old.

"We were farm workers, but I can't imagine we couldn't afford a proper burial."

"Yeah, back then it wouldn't have cost that much."

I'd have filled a thousand crop boxes if that's what it would have taken.

"Was there a funeral service?"

"I'm sure a priest said some things, but that was probably it."

A fingernail scratched the blackboard of my mind. Mom truly didn't know where her son was buried after all. My jaw clenched. I wanted to use a jackhammer to unearth my brother and take him home.

"Listen," Mike continued. "There's a tree in the chapel with bronze leaves inscribed with names of the departed. It's something we just started for families who've lost someone and aren't able to recover the body. Someone who died overseas in the war, for example. You could have your brother's name on one of the leaves."

My thoughts swirled with the wrenching understanding that my brother's body lay in an inconceivable place. What in the world happened? I was sure God had planned for me to find him, but I didn't think it'd be like this.

Weeks later, I returned to see my little brother's memorial at the chapel. The oval-shaped leaf bore his name in large capital letters: PERRY CRUZ. Below, his dates curved: 9–21–60 to 1–18–64. At the top, the words in all caps, LOVED AND NOT FORGOTTEN, rounded over his name like a protective umbrella.

Back home, I ached to know that my brother made it to heaven. I sent a letter to St. Francis Catholic Church in midtown Sacramento requesting that a Wednesday noon mass be dedicated to the memory of my brother.

Martina accompanied me to the lunchtime service.

Father Barry, the senior priest, wore a chocolate-brown robe with a corded rope around his waist. He stepped to the front and paused to smile at me.

He delivered his sermon to our small gathering in a hushed, conversational tone. I paid little attention and just wanted to hear my brother's name. At 12:30 p.m., Father Barry stopped and gazed upward.

"We dedicate this service today to the memory of Perry Cruz, who was taken from this earth at the tender age of three, for reasons known only to God." He straightened and spoke in an even and unhurried tone. "In some cases, the circumstances of a dearly departed remain unknown. The only thing we do know is that he, Perry, exists in the loving arms of our Savior, Lord Jesus. We thank You for taking him into Your care and for him being a blessing during his time here. Amen."

Martina and I began to rise, contented that Father Barry's words for Perry were all we hoped for. But the priest's gaze held me in place.

"Pete, he's looking at you now." Father Barry pointed to the ceiling and spoke with compassion. "Your brother is seated next to Jesus and they both have their eyes on you. Perry says, 'Thank you, big brother.'"

Tears rushed to my eyes. Although at the time I had a limited concept of Christianity, I believed the vision to be true. Perry was in good hands with the Lord, and He helped me to find peace.

Less than a year after one Cruz child was given a proper send-off, another was born into the world.

41

Natalia

"**Just take breaths** like we learned in class," I said to Martina. I reminded myself to breathe as well. I hoped she hadn't seen the concern in my face or heard the waver in my voice.

Martina clamped my hand like Vise-Grips. Her intermittent whimpers left me not knowing what to do.

I had wanted to lead her in Lamaze breathing exercises, but in the stress of the moment, I couldn't remember the process. For me, Lamaze may as well translate to "The Maze." I couldn't find my way.

"Ow! Ooh," Martina wailed. Either the epidural had worn off or she was going further into labor.

In minutes, Dr. Stevens stepped in. She was a confident, agreeable woman who never seemed to be in a hurry.

She glanced at Martina and shot me a look of reassurance.

"Ooh, it hurts," Martina said. I'd never seen her in such pain. I realized my ignorance of the birthing process. I wanted to pull my chair to the corner so I could put on a dunce cap.

Contractions continued with less time between them. In control and patient, Dr. Stevens waited and observed.

Beads of perspiration formed on Martina's forehead like raindrops on lily pads.

Impending fatherhood weighed on my mind. *Please, let our daughter be healthy.* I prayed to an unknown, vague concept of God.

And I squirmed.

"Push. I need you to push for me," Dr. Stevens instructed.

"Aahhhh, Ohh, Oooh," My wife cried out Sesame Street vowel pronunciations.

"C'mon, you can do it," Dr. Stevens said in equal parts demand and encouragement.

Martina grunted. She clenched her jaw, and determination came over her face.

I grasped her hand.

"Push!" Dr. Stevens implored. Then louder still, "Push!" Our baby's doctor no doubt hailed from the Iditarod School of Birthing.

Martina groaned and snorted as if lifting weights for an Olympic gold medal.

Dr. Stevens moved a half step back, stood erect, and smiled in satisfaction.

"There she is," the doctor proclaimed as she held up our crying daughter in both hands.

"Eight o'clock a.m.," Dr. Stevens said.

I had also been born at eight o'clock in the morning.

"Congratulations, Mom," the doctor said. She plopped our baby on top of her mother's stomach.

"Congratulations, Dad."

"Thank you for everything, Dr. Stevens."

Our newborn baby's guttural cries continued.

Martina smiled while her eyes twinkled with joy. She was exhausted. All she could do was lie still and watch Natalia on her stomach.

Natalia lay prone with her face to the side. Her hair was wet with birth fluid, and she continued to bawl. I assumed sleepless nights were in store for her parents.

Natalia lifted her head in what looked like her first attempt at a push-up. She posed like a miniature sphinx.

Our eyes locked on each other, and her cries suspended. For a moment frozen in time, we silently stared at each other. I felt as if her expression was an unmistakable recognition of me.

I'm glad you know who your father is. We have a shared destiny.

The moment broke and she resumed hollering.

42

Full Circle

Dad died less than a year and a half after Natalia's birth.
After his funeral service, we reconvened for his interment at the
Santa Clara Mission Cemetery. His eulogy was still fresh on my mind. I
wondered if I'd weep at his burial.

Afternoon shadows from nearby tombstones resembled outstretched
hands reaching for our dad's open grave.

The priest departed, and the immediate Cruz family members remained seated graveside. Gone was the relief we'd felt from our father's
passing days earlier. Now his departure seemed to weigh on us. In my
mind, any notion of his demise wiping away our past traumas and hurts
appeared as empty as the open hole in the ground. We each sat alone with
our thoughts.

"We're here to lower the casket, if that is okay." A young man and his
coworker stood next to me.

"Sure. Do you need us to leave?"

"No, no. Stay if you'd like." No one moved. I wanted to see Dad
lowered into the earth and out of sight. It seemed we all sought the same
thing—closure.

The workers kneeled at each end of the casket and cranked levers to
lower the coffin. The casket was laden with bouquets received from family
members, friends, and coworkers. I stood to peer into the hole.

I thought about how much I had toiled for Dad. Laying him to rest
would be the last job I'd do for him.

As Buster rose from his seat to join me, someone gagged and choked. I turned behind me. Mom struggled to contain herself. It was the only sorrow I'd seen from her in the days since her husband's death. It looked as if she didn't want to cry. Maybe she followed the same family rule I did, that it was impermissible to express care or concern. I wondered if she had grieved in her private moments.

Buster clutched a Coke can and tossed Dad's favorite beverage inside. The soda can clanged on top of the coffin. Its pop top burst, fizzing and spraying over the flowers.

"That represents his final outburst," I said. A fitting tribute.

The grounds workers left. Cookie and Penny stayed in their seats and wept. Mom sat with her head bowed and a forlorn expression on her face.

Mimi stepped forward and stood between Buster and me. Tears streaked her face like droplets from a rain-splashed window. Scoop and Pat rose from their seats and took places in line with us. Finally, Cookie and Penny joined us, while Mom remained seated.

Mimi clutched her handheld cassette player and then pressed the On button. Strains of melodic acoustic guitar broke the silence and Eric Clapton sang "Tears in Heaven."

We stood shoulder to shoulder, the usual suspects in a lineup alongside our father's grave.

Mimi grasped my hand, and everyone followed, joining hands like a string of paper dolls.

The lyrics were poignant. If I were to see Dad in heaven, would he know my name? Would Jesus keep him in check? Would He whisper in Dad's ear and advise him not to say anything disparaging?

Would I recognize Dad? I'd only known my father as a glowering, raging monster, pacing like an angry bull, ready to charge. I couldn't imagine him any other way.

Except for Buster and me, everyone continued to weep.

I wanted to cry but couldn't. My resentment was too great. My crying would represent sentimentality and forgiveness. I had none for him. There were no tears.

How it came to pass that Perry and Dad were buried in the same cemetery was never questioned, but it seemed too much of a coincidence. Their graves were about thirty yards apart.

"There will never be a better time to tell them that we've found Perry's grave," I said to Pat.

"Listen, everybody," Pat turned to our family and paused for their attention. "Peewee has something to tell you."

"I want to let you know that Perry is also buried here. I found him last year. Pat had followed up about six months later and discovered him here also." I pointed to the chapel in the distance. "Let's go over there. I can give you the details. Plus, there's something I want to show you."

The large oak door of the chapel opened to rows of wooden pews. The silence and stillness resonated reverence and respect for a God unfamiliar to most of us.

Family members shuffled into the first few rows. Mom sat in a back row by herself.

"Last year I got ahold of Perry's death certificate that listed this cemetery as his burial place." My finger jabbed down for emphasis. "He died of something called 'hemosiderosis,' which pertains to a blood disorder of the lungs. I guess there was something to his licking the rust off those old farm implements at Mabury Road."

Mom turned to the side as if she were staring at something across the pew. I couldn't tell if she was listening or had chosen not to listen.

I desired to say only what I knew, not to accuse or induce guilt. I had little understanding of what goes through a mother's mind after losing a three-year-old child. Maybe the pain had been too overwhelming to keep his photos or even say his name again.

As usual, she sat in the back row as unreadable as a mystery novel with its last pages torn out.

"He doesn't have a grave," I said. "What I mean is there's no headstone. His was a county burial, which is for families that can't afford one. After this, we can walk over to where he is. Because he doesn't have a gravestone, they offered to have his name printed on a leaf here."

I walked to the wall where the art-deco styled tree was covered with bronze leaves.

These leaves are for families who've lost someone and weren't able to recover the body or have a gravestone."

There were many more since the last time I had visited. "His is right here."

Family members lined up to look closely at the leaf. Mom viewed it from several feet away.

After everyone looked at it, we pushed our way through the chapel back into the bright sunlight.

It was a short stroll to the hedgerow along the roadway at Perry's location.

"I think he's about here." I stamped my foot on the asphalt.

"Here?" Cookie leaned toward me.

"Yes, here. Under here."

"Under here?" Her brow furrowed as she sidled away.

"Mike, at the office, told me you had written things in chalk here and had tied balloons to the hedges," Pat said.

"There were flowers too. And I gave Perry a bear." I parted the leaves of the bushes. His bear remained secure within the branches. The bear's white, billowy fur had become gray, worn, and matted.

"Aww, there he is," Cookie said.

"That was nice of you to do a remembrance for him," Penny added.

"Good job," Scoop said.

Scoop articulated his words in a hushed, neutral tone. During our upbringing, his "good job" was loaded with sarcasm, usually after Dad had smacked me.

Now as adults, Scoop's pronouncement had evolved into a legitimate compliment.

43

Fatherhood Fail

"**Y**ou're so precious," Martina cooed to our three-year-old daughter.

With a beer in hand, I listened from our adjoining family room while unwinding from work.

"Would you like to buy a vowel?" Pat Sajak asked on TV's *Wheel of Fortune*.

"I love you so much," Martina said to Natalia.

Inside of me, fear and sadness descended on the three-year-old child that I once was. Suppressed memories of abandonment and neglect surfaced.

What about me? Nobody cares about me. The little boy that was me gazed from within. His deep, mournful eyes pleaded for attention.

"You're my precious little girl," Martina continued.

Like touching a hot stove burner, anger jolted me off the sofa. I'd show them. A young boy shouldn't be left helpless and neglected.

Nobody cares about me lit a blazing fuse. The little boy found in me an adult avenger. Grown-up me would handle it.

Into the living room I marched. Just as I'd thought, mother held daughter and behaved in ways I'd never known from my own mother.

Fear of abandonment struck my inner being like a thunderstorm, saturating me in a torrential downpour of anguish and fury.

With a beer bottle still in my hand, I flung it across the floor like a rolled-up newspaper delivery. The bottle skidded and bounced bottom first across the carpet. Foam spurted and sprayed from its top. It came to rest, and its remaining contents soaked into the rug.

Facing my wife and daughter, I stared wide-eyed—shocked at what I'd done.

They gawked. Martina's eyes remained unblinking. Her lips parted, but she said nothing.

Natalia cried and turned to her mother for protection. Had her toddler mind grasped that her father had become unhinged?

What had I done? Why? I hovered over the bottle that my accusing eyes wanted to identify as the source of my anger.

I stared at the damp crime scene as confusion clouded my mind.

Avoiding eye contact with Martina, I walked to the kitchen, heavy with shame. After disposing the bottle under the sink, I trudged to the carpet with paper towels and dabbed at wet spots. No amount of cleaning could make up for the mess I'd made.

I had no explanation to offer my wife, so I went up the stairs. Each step was like ascending to the gallows.

Anguished over the destruction I had brought to my family, I lay on my bed.

What have I done? Have I become my father? I twisted on my bed, wrestling with the fact that I had behaved like Dad in front of my daughter—again.

I turned to my side and hugged my knees to my stomach. Remorse and shame enveloped me.

As illogical as it sounds in retrospect, I reasoned the only way to avoid the same situation would be if I lived with Natalia somewhere else. Then I wouldn't be subject to uncontrolled outbursts.

I resolved to move out.

Martina and I never spoke about my bottle-hurling incident. She never asked about it either. I suppose we feared bringing up its ugliness. Maybe it was easier to keep it hidden.

Weeks later, without any explanation, I announced, "I'm going to move." Martina descended the stairs into the family room where I waited on the sofa. She placed her foot on the last step of the stairs and nodded. A single large teardrop slid down her face.

"I rented an apartment. I'm moving out by the first of the month."

For ten years of a roller-coaster ride through my eruptions and emotional instability, she'd done the utmost to preserve our marriage. It wasn't her fault that I turned out to be a man with a fractured psyche. From the beginning, I should have realized that I didn't know how to be a husband.

I was grateful that we had established a fifty-fifty custody arrangement for Natalia. Our daughter would stay with either parent on alternate weeks. I wanted to remain a significant part of my daughter's life. I'd read that a father's absence led his daughter to seek other men, usually older, to fill the void. I hoped my daughter would not do so out of a need I'd created.

My biggest ambition was not to advance in my career or to amass wealth, power, or fame. I desired to be a good father.

"Okay," I said at her doorway. "Time to go to sleep." I waited for Natalia to get to her bed and then switched off the light. It was our first night in our apartment.

I retreated to my bedroom and flung myself on the bed. I lay against my pillow to read one of the books I kept at my nightstand.

A slight noise crept into the air. It sounded something like, "Ah, ah." Immersed in a spy novel, I didn't make out the source of the noise.

The sound continued. I raised my head to hear better. It came from my daughter's room.

I rushed to turn on her light. She sat on her bed, clutching her knees to her chest.

When I hurried to her side, she continued to emit a faint "Ah." A pained expression covered her face.

"What's wrong?" She didn't answer.

"Does something hurt?" Still nothing.

After her next "Ah," I was dumbfounded.

Was she afraid of the dark as I had been at her age? I pondered whether to leave the light on or dash to the hardware store for a night-light.

The inner boy in me suggested Natalia couldn't sleep in the dark, alone in a strange room. I put my arm around her shoulders and gently squeezed.

"Do you want to sleep in my bed?"

She peered at me with round and sorrowful eyes and nodded yes.

Through Natalia's first three years, her mother had put her to bed. My fathering style amounted to the one I had learned from my own parents, which was put yourself to bed. I had assumed my daughter would do the same. Years later, it dawned on me that I could've tucked her in, sat with her, read her a bedtime story, and even kissed her on the forehead goodnight.

It occurred to me that I didn't know what I didn't know.

I had failed in my marriage, which concluded with the thrown beer bottle. The first night Natalia and I were together, I was hoping I had moved on from the situation. But I hadn't. At least I realized she was afraid of being alone in the dark.

There was so much I needed to learn about how to be a good father.

44

Darkness Revisited

"There's a suicide note here." A man's voice penetrated the void.
I felt as if I'd failed at everything in my life. I even failed with suicide. The pills and alcohol weren't enough to do me in.

"Male, forty, responsive," the man's voice continued. Consciousness washed over the shores of my mind.

"Let's take him to Sutter General." A woman's voice sounded, then receded into the fog.

Vibrations beneath me vied for attention as I was transported outside. Morning light and the cool air stirred me to consciousness. I strained to open my eyes to take in the situation. My elderly next-door neighbor stood nearby. Her usual friendly face was now etched with concern.

The gurney jostled into the back of the ambulance like a spoon in a silverware drawer. The transport's rear doors closed with a sudden thud. Wakefulness faded into a dim memory of a *Twilight Zone* episode called "A Stop At Willoughby." Its eerie final scene showed a hearse door slam shut from the Willoughby morgue.

At the hospital, a medical assistant wiped my mouth, cleaning remnants of activated charcoal that helped empty my stomach's contents. A menacing wave pounded the shoreline of my psyche. Dad's voice filled my thoughts: "Isn't that something? You can't do anything right."

"I'm a chaplain," a visitor said. My ER station's enclosure was nothing more than a shower curtain. I didn't know what a chaplain was, other than a religious title. He could've been Charlie Chaplin for all I cared. I'd have been fine if he had remained mute.

"Would you like me to say a prayer for you?" he asked.

"Why would I want you to do that? It doesn't matter to me." I stared at the patterns in the ceiling tiles. He lingered a moment and then departed.

"I'm a social worker," my next guest said. She was a Hispanic who appeared to be in her forties. I hoped she hadn't been assigned to my case based on my Spanish surname. I'd been to enough auto dealerships where they'd trot out an Asian or Hispanic salesman closest to my age who'd try to ingratiate me with his brotherly sales pitch. I half expected her to greet me with "Hola, Pedro. Me llamo es . . ."

Her face revealed caution. Was she afraid I'd tear off my backless hospital robe and run through the hallways? Or maybe she felt uneasy with my sneer, which I hoped rivaled that of Jack Nicholson's in *One Flew Over the Cuckoo's Nest.*

"What happens next?" I questioned in a manner matching my dark mood.

"I'm just going to ask you some questions to assess your frame of mind."

"My frame of mind is I just tried to kill myself, but I'm still here. How do you think my frame of mind is?" My jaw tightened and my upper lip curled in a snarl.

"Does that bother you?"

"Yes; it means I failed. I pride myself on being able to accomplish what I set my mind to, good or bad. Where did I go wrong? Maybe I shouldn't have called 9-1-1 at the last second."

"You didn't go wrong anywhere. You did right. I'm glad you're still here."

After she jotted my sarcasm-laden answers onto her clipboard, she said, "You'll be transported to Sutter Center for Psychiatry (SCP). It's a nice facility. The staff are well regarded. You'll be in good hands."

SCP's modern architectural design included olive-green exterior paneling and a well maintained and tasteful landscape. If I hadn't known better, I would have mistaken the mental health facility for a gated townhome community.

My first stay at a psychiatric hospital was a voluntary admission twelve years earlier with a three-day hold. Now forty-three years old, I was an involuntary admit for what became three weeks.

When I strolled the grounds, I fixed my gaze at a group of stadium lights in the distance. They belonged to the Sacramento State University football field. I pondered the time I had spent there as a student more than twenty years earlier. They had been some of the best years of my life. Now my life was derailed.

Counseling was scheduled for me every other day, and I participated in the institution's group therapy, educational clinics, and recreational activities. The SCP offered me a break from life, but it was also like a *brake* because my life had come to an abrupt halt.

The art therapy instructor pointed to a table: "Take the art supplies we have here and draw whatever comes to mind. The quality of your artwork has no bearing on this exercise. When you're finished, you can share your work with the rest of us, but it's not required."

Crayons and felt pens would show on the black sheet of construction paper I selected. I sketched a bull, which covered the full page. His chest was inflated like a massive helium balloon. Fearsome horns aimed outward. His red eyes glowered and his nostrils flared with steaming jets of fury.

The drawing represented a recurring dream. In it, I darted through a narrow jungle path while the wild, angry beast pursued me. The jungle was so dense that I couldn't leave the trail and had no choice but to pitch forward. The mad bull snorted as his thunderous gallops closed in. I knew the bull would soon impale me on his horns or trample me underfoot. At the point when the bull was about to overtake me, I jumped and grabbed the overhead vines and swung my body upward. The bull charged underneath; his horns grazed the underside of my pant legs. The bull hurtled on, enraged that he barely missed me.

Each time, I awoke shaking in a sweat, sometimes screaming out, but always gasping for breath.

In my sketch, I drew myself as an inch-high character cornered at the bottom of the paper. My arms were outstretched, pleading to the bull to stop.

I didn't need the art therapist to interpret my drawing—I knew who the bull was.

45

Return to Work

During my stay at SCP, social security disability benefits were approved and a medical leave of absence from my job was secured.

After my release, I attended appointments with mental health professionals such as psychiatrists, psychologists, and social workers. They assessed my mental health to determine if I could eventually return to work.

My daughter, Natalia, was not yet school age. During the day she stayed with me, and she returned to her mom's in the evening. I often brought her to various playgrounds in the Sacramento area where she played on the monkey bars and swings. Sometimes we sat at a coffee shop along with other young mothers. Conversation never occurred between us because I felt out of place. I felt I should be at work. As weeks turned to months, I exercised at the gym each morning. Natalia enjoyed the gym's childcare program. I adhered to a weight-training program designed with exercises off my feet, which continued to be plagued with pain. My workouts were the only activity that provided a sense of accomplishment. For the most part, I drifted. Aimless. Hopeless and helpless. A man with no future.

"I've been thinking about going back to work," I announced at one of my weekly counseling appointments, which I had attended for about a year.

Always tired, Georgia, my regular therapist, possessed the verve of a metronome. But when she confirmed, "You're thinking about going back to work?" she acted as if she'd just won the lottery.

"Yes. That's what I said."

"That's certainly good news. What's brought you to this decision?" Her job had been a ho-hum task of monitoring my mental state and recording my lack of readiness for work. My sessions with her were always monotonous and lackluster.

"My daughter started kindergarten, and although I sometimes volunteer in her class, my life has amounted to lifting weights and sitting in coffee shops. There's got to be more to life than that."

She turned to my file. "You've been off for two and a half years now." For the first time, a tinge of enthusiasm infused her voice. "Please continue. I'm listening."

When I used to work, a to-do list was my method for accomplishing tasks. I'd now become listless.

"I'm thinking it'd be good to be in a work environment and be productive again." I peered at the floor to gather my thoughts. "I need to be around people too. I enjoy cracking jokes. It's hard to be funny without an audience."

She eyed me with a look of a stern schoolteacher. After my being such a somber, disinterested client, she probably thought I was the unfunniest person she'd ever met. I suppressed an urge to rise to my feet, wave my arms in unison, and blurt out, "I'm a wild and crazy guy," in my best Steve Martin imitation. I thought better of it, though, fearing she had SCP on speed dial.

"We certainly can make that work. I'll file the paperwork immediately." She scribbled on her clipboard like a student cramming for a midterm. "We can get you back to work by the first of the month." My lower lip unhinged. *What's with her sudden uptick in energy? Does she get a commission for removing me from her rolls?*

She may have been as tired of me as I was of her. Nonetheless, it was time for me to enter back into society.

———

After filling out reinstatement papers, unease about my impending placement with a new unit and new job duties weighed on my mind.

My first step into a chilly stairwell reminded me of how I'd enter a swimming pool. I immersed myself a little at a time, attempting to get used to the cold. My reentry into employment waters wouldn't be like that. I'd launch myself in all at once. With each step down the stairs, the cold reality of rejoining the workforce after two and a half years made me shudder.

While I went down the steps, someone came up. Slender with long black hair, she stopped several steps below me.

"Hi. Are you the person who's going to work for us?"

"If you mean at the Administration and Program Control Office (APCO), then yes, that would be me." She looked faintly familiar and I assumed I'd seen her around the building prior to my medical leave. "How'd you know? Have I met you before?"

"I saw you walk by last week when you met with our boss, Kate."

"Oh, yeah." I closed the remaining steps between us and extended my hand. "My name's Pete."

"I'm Beth. Kate's nice. She's a good supervisor."

"She was one of my students when I taught Introduction to Supervision."

"Oh, I see. We're a good group. There are five of us in the administration section." Her smile and ease of expression comforted me. Trust resonated in her words.

"That's good to know," I said.

On my first day of work, I discovered Beth occupied the office next to mine. It turned out Beth was a Filipina. She didn't have an attitude like others in my culture who saw me as too Americanized. She hailed from a small province in the southern Philippines and spoke an obscure dialect.

In time, I came to regard her like a sister.

My practical-joke humor returned when I made a paper pyramid for her birthday.

"What's this?" she asked.

"It's not big enough to be a mountain, so it's a hill," I explained. "Today, each time you enter or exit your office, you'll have to step over it. It'll be your personal reminder that you're over the hill. Get it? Over the hill?"

———

Over the years, Beth became my closest confidant. We talked about the good and bad and peaks and valleys of our lives. I trusted her enough to disclose almost everything about my difficult upbringing and how it continued to affect me in adulthood.

During breaks or lunchtimes, she read the Bible, but I thought nothing of it. Once in a while, she mentioned her Christian viewpoint, but I dismissed whatever she said.

I continued to struggle with life. I missed many workdays due to bouts of depression and had used all my sick and vacation leave. With any more absences, I faced having my time docked and my paycheck reduced.

Beth was aware of how difficult life was for me.

"I want to tell you about the God I know," she said.

I wasn't ready.

46

Thirty for Thirty

"**This is my** little black book," Stephen said as he seated himself at his kitchen table. My buddy's mannerisms always seemed to suggest that he was letting me in on a secret.

"Is that so?" I replied. "Whatcha got? Phone numbers for your mom and two sisters?" I ribbed him like most guys do to each other about our supposed prowess with the opposite sex.

"I have everybody's address and phone number in here," he said while he wrote in my newest location. "You're the only person I know whose address I have in pencil. You're like a nomad or a gypsy." An image of myself wearing a headscarf came to mind.

Out of curiosity, when I returned home, Stephen's comments prompted me to figure out exactly how many times I'd moved since I had left home in 1976.

My task was simple because I usually kept records beyond their usefulness.

My pen clunked to the desk after I surveyed the list I had compiled. I had changed residences thirty times in as many years! My hands tented over my nose and mouth. I bit my lip with the realization that I had moved an average of once per year for three decades.

Like an interrupted TV program, breaking news scrolled through my head: "Pete Cruz is indeed a nomad. Stay tuned for comments from Captain Obvious."

As I pondered the places I'd lived, it occurred to me that I was probably looking for home. Perhaps I didn't know what home looked like, which may have kept me on the move. Some moves were temporary housing during college. Others seemed to be moves for the sake of moving. Some residences lasted six months, and none lasted longer than three years. I'd even bought five houses.

While I clasped my hands behind my head like an armchair psychologist, it occurred to me there existed an ongoing situation at my boyhood home where the other shoe was bound to drop. I missed my neighbors, but did I keep moving due to deep-seated fears of trouble on the horizon? Other times, I may have left before I felt too comfortable in the neighborhood. Not wanting to let my guard down, had I rejected my neighbors before they could reject me?

With my amateur psychologist hat on, I suspected that after the duress of growing up, the fight-or-flight response stayed activated.

Beyond my mindless compulsion to fight, I must have been in perpetual flight.

47

Apples from the Tree

Natalia and I settled on our seats across from each other for dinner. The kitchen table was set, and we helped ourselves to rice, green beans, and pork chops. I gazed out the window overlooking the street while Natalia sat with her back to it.

Natalia's glass of cola sat beside her plate. My hand surrounded my usual dinnertime bottle of beer. Natalia took small, measured bites. On occasion, she took a sip from her glass and carefully set it back down. She dined in silence with her eyes fixed on her plate. Not once did she look at me.

I had hoped our evening meals would be a time where she'd share about her day in junior high school. It never happened. And on this day, I finally took notice that she was always quiet.

"Why aren't you talking?" I asked.

Her eyes upraised and her mouth paused in mid-chew. She resumed eating without reply.

Did she not hear me? Wasn't she feeling well? Maybe she was mad at me.

"Why aren't you talking?" I asked again, more forcefully.

She paused to glance at me and uplifted a shoulder.

Was that a shrug of defiance? Of uncertainty? Or a sign she didn't care?

"Is there something I said or did?" My words scratched like sandpaper. I was Dirty Harry asking her to "Go ahead, make my day."

"I don't know." Her bottom lip quivered and she frowned. Simply translated, she wanted me to leave her alone.

Her sad eyes drooped and her bottom lip continued to tremble.

What happened to make her so afraid to talk to me? How long had this been going on?

I never talked to my dad either. Whenever he asked me a question, it felt like an interrogation. He'd stand over me like a prosecuting attorney conducting a cross-examination. I divulged as little as possible, not wanting to invite further hurtful comments.

My daughter squirmed in front of me—a sure sign that she feared me as I had feared my dad. A sinking feeling in my stomach gave way to self-realization: my behavior toward my daughter was the same as Dad's conduct toward me. I had raised a daughter fearful of me.

What's more, her unsmiling face and refusal to converse suggested a future like my present, grappling with depression. *How was that possible?* I lived my life thinking that in no way was I like my father.

I'd attempted to fix myself through years of counseling. I'd read countless self-help books and attended numerous psychological workshops. Yet until that day at dinner, I couldn't see that the apple hadn't fallen far from the tree. I'd become my dad.

It wasn't supposed to be this way.

The thought of fathering a daughter who'd want nothing to do with me tore into my being. To the pit of my stomach, I ached to be the dad my father wasn't. *How could I change? Hadn't I tried everything? To whom or what could I turn for help?*

48

Job Transfers

"**T**his is Charlotte." My immediate supervisor always answered her phone after two rings. Charlotte had replaced Kate, who had been promoted to a director position.

"Hi, boss. This is Pete." It was another workday, eight o'clock in the morning. "I can't make it today."

"Okay," she said. She'd stopped asking me for reasons, although it was within her rights. She understood that an "I can't make it today" call from me meant I was struggling against depression and wasn't faking a cough or headache to stay home. I couldn't get out of bed, let alone leave my house. What I would have given to have an actual physical ailment!

"I'm sorry," I said. Shame set in.

"No, it's all right. We'll miss you. You have your friends here."

I advised her of the status of my projects, meetings, or deadlines.

"There's nothing that can't wait until you get back. Just know we all care about you. Call me later if you want to talk," she said.

After I hung up, a blanket of guilt and humiliation covered me.

About a year after my return to work, it had been that way for me. Several times I had told Charlotte, "Getting out of bed to go to work is the hardest thing I do all day."

It wasn't because I didn't like my job. My job gave me a sense of productivity and accomplishment.

During the alternate weeks when Natalia was home, I was usually able to drive her to school. From there I managed to go to work; a few times I was filled with dread and went back home.

Alone in my house, depression was like a giant invisible hand that held me in bed.

Rising from bed took up to an hour. I'd try to talk myself into it during the first part of the hour. For the second half, I attempted to throw off the covers and slide my legs to the floor. When that didn't work, I raised my legs upward similar to doing leg lifts at the gym and hoped to swing them to the side. Instead, my legs repeatedly fell back down on the bed.

I glared at the clock, dreading the passing of time. As a final act of self-determination, I roused myself into a sitting position, stood to get dressed, then drooped in front of the bathroom mirror to swipe at my head with a hairbrush.

I often drove to work unsure and disheartened, then entered my office embarrassed that I'd gotten out of bed only half an hour earlier.

On Saturdays, I wondered how I had been able to get through the week. On Sundays, I mentally readied myself for the coming week. Another leave of absence or application for disability benefits was out of the question. I feared time at home without anything to look forward to could lead to a dark road from which I'd never recover.

After some time, I rationalized a transfer to another department or a return to my job as a trainer might restore my life to what it was before I had left the workforce for two and a half years.

I parked on a side street a few blocks from a high-rise building in downtown Sacramento. As I walked along the sidewalk, dread tugged at me like an impatient mother hurrying her adolescent through a grocery store aisle.

Fear stood with me at the elevator. I took gulping breaths. It was day three of reporting to my new job, and my anxiety hadn't lessened.

When I stepped off the elevator, I pasted on a smile.

I didn't know anyone at my new place of employment. I was afraid I couldn't learn my new job fast enough. I worried I'd be criticized for not understanding anything and would be considered not good enough.

Past insecurities spilled forward. My self-doubts were too much. I feared strangers and new environments. The new work environment enclosed me like a Chinese finger trap. The more I pulled, the harder it was to get out.

The start of day four wasn't any different than one through three. Driving there, my palms were wet as I gripped the steering wheel in a futile attempt to control my anxiety. As I drove the city streets searching for a parking space, I imagined a cartoon hand swinging a giant Monopoly card that read, "Do Not Pass Go, Do Not Collect $200, Go Directly to Jail."

My fears imprisoned me, and I could drive no farther. I turned in the opposite direction and drove back home.

"This is Charlotte." My old boss answered after two rings.

Prior to phoning her, I first called the supervisor at my new job to tell her I had a headache and couldn't come in.

"Hi, this is Pete."

"Hey, Pete. How's the new job going?" She seemed happy to hear from me.

"That's why I'm calling. Has my old job been filled yet?"

"No. I was going to get together with Beth this afternoon to see if the duty statement needed updating. Why?"

"I'm having trouble adjusting."

"Is it the job?"

"No. It's me. Do you think it'd be okay if I came back?" I hoped to grab a get-out-of-jail-free card from the pile.

"Oh, you know we miss you. You sure you don't need a few more days to see if it'll work out?"

"I'm at home now. I couldn't go in today. I made it all the way downtown before I had to turn back. I can't go anymore."

Charlotte knew the Pete who wrestled with depression. He was a far cry from the usually capable and efficient employee.

"Let me talk to the chief. I don't think she'll have a problem. She likes you. And then I'll call personnel to see what the process is for getting you back here. It might take a few days, but I'll phone you this afternoon to let you know."

A week later, I was graciously allowed back to my old job. I was safe again, doing a job I knew well, and around people I trusted.

I lived a life littered with potholes. Where could I find a smooth and level path?

49

A Grave Visit

A long the cement walkway that divided the cemetery's separate areas, stone benches covered by wood trellises faced the gravesites. Dad's flat marker gravestone would be located four or five spaces from the footpath. A faint breeze wafted through the grounds.

When Dad was alive, he seemed to appreciate my stopping by, although few sentences were spoken between us. He made me something to eat, and our visits rarely lasted an hour. But now I made the trip from Sacramento because I had something to say to him.

As I made my way toward the end of the cemetery, some graves had bouquets that stood upright in their containers and others laid flat on the grass. An unwrapped candy bar lay on one plot, and an opened can of beer on another.

Dad's headstone was rose pink. CRUZ was inscribed within a rectangle at the top center. A smaller frame contained his full name and dates. A similar space next to it remained empty for Mom's passing. At the bottom, the gravestone read, "At Rest with God." It seemed a fitting epitaph because when he was alive, he was anything but at rest. I visited him because I still sought what I believed he never found—peace while living.

It had been a while since I'd last been there. The stone hadn't been washed or swept. Small crevice lines appeared over the once-smooth finish and were filled in by black earth. They reminded me of his grim and fearsome facial expressions.

The flower holders on each side sat empty. I wondered if they'd ever contained a floral gift. It didn't look as if any of my brothers or sisters visited. In death as in life, his kids didn't call on him.

"You did this, Dad," I uttered aloud, surprised by my thought made vocal. "You made it so we don't want to visit you."

Like him, his tombstone appeared cold, unforgiving, and unfeeling. Was he listening? With my hands balled on my hips, I turned my head to the sky.

"I've tried so hard. I wanted to be a good son. I did everything you asked, most of it perfectly. When everyone stopped coming by to see you, I still came." My voice began to break. "I just wanted your approval, but I never got it." Tears stung my eyes, just like our relationship.

"I've had a difficult life. I've been depressed since childhood. I can't seem to live in one place. I couldn't transfer to another job. I have chronic pain. I don't think I have it in me to marry again."

Perhaps out of habit to never show him my pain, I turned away from the stone that was him. Tears soaked my eyes. "What did you do to me? I've spent most of my life trying to hold it together. It's taken so much out of me just to survive you. I should've, I could've been doing other things."

Through my sniffles, I peered in the direction of my little brother Perry's grave. Sometimes I considered that he escaped where I could not.

"What gets me is, if you made it to heaven, you're probably a different person there, and you have a good relationship with Perry. It kills me that I'm doing to my own daughter what you did to me."

My teeth clenched and my jaw hardened.

"I don't know what I'm doing. You can't help me because you're not even here. There's really nothing more to say."

Trudging to a nearby bench, I sat and gathered myself before the drive back to northern California.

Hoping that I might detect his unearthly presence, I gazed at Dad's grave. I wanted an apology, or even an answer to help me with my unraveled life.

On the other end of the bench, someone had left a small ceramic figurine, about three inches high, of an infant boy with wings. He was in a sitting position with stubby legs hanging off the edge of the bench.

I pondered the figurine and made a silent request: *Can you help him?*

I placed the angel boy on the headstone.

Then I went home.

50

Pushed Buttons

"**A**fter I tried to go to my new workplace, I went back home and called my old boss to ask for my job back." I recounted recent events to Iko Miyazaki, the latest psychotherapist and a protégé of Satsuki's. "I can't believe I couldn't make a new career move."

"That's PTSD," she commented. She announced it as if it were plain fact.

I had trouble seeing how combat veterans who suffer flashbacks related to my situation. I'd never seen anyone get shot or blown to smithereens. I wondered if she noticed the faraway look in my eyes. She didn't elaborate, and I felt foolish to ask about what seemed an obvious observation. *What's PTSD?*

After some thought, I concluded it was a given that my past affected my present. I grew up having to face Dad first thing in the morning. Maybe from him I learned to dread facing the world. I recalled the fears and anxieties I'd experienced when going to a new school or at events where I didn't know anybody. *Was that why I couldn't go to a new job?* There seemed to be an unseen button within me that got pushed.

"My foot pain is the worst thing that's ever happened to me," I declared to Iko.

"What, not your dad?" My therapist glanced at her notepad, and her eyes narrowed.

"My dad's dead." I spoke in a grave manner, not intending to deadpan my words. "Pain in my feet is something I live with every day. It's the first reminder I have when I step out of bed in the morning. Since its onset, my life totally changed. I used to be active. Tennis and basketball were part of my identity. I used to jog to relieve stress. Now I have to parcel out my ability to get groceries or do yardwork."

"Have doctors been able to help you?"

"Years ago, I spent at least a month with the UC Davis Pain Management Clinic. They referred me to various departments within the Med Center where I was tested for things like gout and neuropathy. I had MRIs done to look for structural or nerve damage. They found nothing."

I drew in a breath, then continued.

"One thing I found noteworthy was when I stepped off the examining table to the bare floor. Bells started ringing on the machine I was hooked up to and a nurse came running in."

"Is that me?" I asked her. I felt fine.

"She said I had set off an alert because my blood pressure reading was high. It makes me think that whenever I'm on my feet, pain causes my blood pressure to spike."

"So you have high blood pressure?" Iko asked.

"Yes, it's alarming." I reminded myself of the seriousness of our discussion. There was no need to chuckle about a pun.

"There's nothing they could do for you?"

"No. This has been going on for over twenty years, so I keep hoping medical science will advance to a point where I can recover."

"Have you ever thought that since the medical community hasn't found its source or remedy, that the two could be connected?"

"Which two?"

"Your dad and your chronic pain. On a psychological level, it is possible for the two to be connected."

"Years ago, I saw another counselor for a short time. She was more New Age. She said, 'It's as if your feet are saying, "I can't stand this anymore. I can't take another step. I can't move forward."' I used to read a lot of New Age books. What she said made a lot of sense."

"Unresolved and unexpressed anger will manifest itself physically in different ways," Iko said.

Was she right?

Pushed Buttons

In an effort to deal with PTSD, I obtained approval from my insurance carrier to receive a relatively new therapy, Eye Movement Desensitization Reprocessing (EMDR), in conjunction with my regular counseling sessions with Iko. EMDR boasted a success rate with military veterans upward of 85 percent.

I attended weekly appointments with Mr. Carlson. He'd take five minutes to set up a light bar on top of a tripod that pulsed horizontal bars of light from left to right at continuous intervals for my eyes to follow. Mr. Carlson said little before, during, or after my forty-minute sessions. With the exception of my initial intake, at subsequent sessions he didn't ask about my past or present mental state.

After several months of my staring at the light bar, he never let me know if I showed signs of progress. I often wondered if I should've gone back to school to make easy money like he seemed to be doing.

My time with Mr. Carlson brought to mind images of a white T-shirted Simon Cowell during *American Idol* auditions. Simon would poke his pen between his lips prior to stating his observations. "Mr. Carlson," he said, "this is a bit like ordering a hamburger and only getting the bun. My advice is if you're what's offered in EMDR specialization—stop." His British lilt underlined his remarks while he smirked and grinned.

"Yo, dawg. This is not good." I pictured Randy Jackson agreeing.

At my next appointment, I expressed to Mr. Carlson, "I think I've gotten a lot better. I'd like to stop."

"Yes, I think you've gotten a lot better," he said. How he arrived at that conclusion, I'll never know.

Nothing was farther from the truth.

51

In Line with God

The smack of volleyballs resounded throughout the San Jose Convention Center. Shrill referee whistles punctuated loud cheers from spectators surrounding each court. Before the start of my daughter's second-round tournament match, I discovered a quiet and subdued Starbucks coffee shop within the edge of the center's complex. No one was around except a lone barista.

"Do you have any questions?" The librarian-like barista stood by to await my order.

"Is a tall the same as a small and is a grande medium size? It sounds like it should be extra large."

"The tall is a small and grande is our medium size. Venti is a large."

The hushed environment eased my hurry, allowing time to decide my order. A few times the barista glanced past my shoulder.

After a while, something stirring behind me provoked my attention, and I turned around. A line numbering at least fifteen customers had formed after me and trailed into the hallway. I quickly ordered coffee and a pastry, embarrassed by my dawdling at the counter, taking all the time in the world to make up my mind.

First in line often happened to me. I'd arrive at places like coffee shops, fast-food restaurants, markets, and banks to find myself first or second in line. Natalia had witnessed these occurrences many times.

"People should hire you to get a shorter place in line," she said.

"The businesses should hire *me* because customers seem to appear out of nowhere once I'm inside."

The only rule seemed to be to not expect it to happen. I'd have to enter each establishment humbled and unaware.

While seated at a small table, I sneaked glances at the line of customers, not wanting anyone to see my moisture-brimmed eyes. I tilted my head down, pretending preoccupation with stirring my coffee.

In a coffee shop at a convention center in the city of my birth, standing in line, an activity most take for granted, made me ponder. The short or non-existent queues and wait times happened so often that they had to be more than coincidence. *But why? How? Was a higher power watching over me?* Until then, I'd always attributed the no-waiting lines to dumb luck and coincidence. Regularly, lines that suddenly formed behind me, even when I didn't dawdle, caused me to stare back in wonder.

The lines seemed to be controlled by a force beyond my understanding. I believed in an infinite, incomprehensible God who created the universe, but this controlling intelligence with the lines seemed personal. His favor seemed to be bestowed on me, at least when it came to walking into businesses. I wondered if there were a God who cared about me, a God who knew the hardships I'd experienced with chronic pain in my feet. I wrestled with the thought that there could be no other explanation than the possible existence of God.

52

Meltdown

Shoes struck my bedroom wall and fell to the floor. Marshaling every bit of strength, another flew from me and thudded. I went to the wall, picked up my shoes, and returned to the pitcher's mound. Again, I threw another footwear fastball, fueled by surging anger, my life once again wronged.

It was 11:00 p.m. on a school night. Natalia's bed lay adjacent on the other side of the wall.

She stirred.

I wanted her to remain awake and fearful of my next move. I was angry at her. I believed she had disrespected me.

I sat on the edge of my bed and drew air deep into my lungs—not from fatigue, but because I was Godzilla and breathed fire. Stomach acids churned and stewed my outrage.

I couldn't even remember what exactly had set me off. Preceding my explosive fury, somewhere and sometime, my daughter had ignored or disregarded me.

As my closest family, Natalia had unknowingly pushed my panic button. The early childhood dread etched in my psyche tried to cope with not being paid attention to. Emotions of feeling small, unheard, and insignificant triggered my defense mechanism. Anger vaulted high to protect me.

I hadn't slept the remainder of the night, and I doubt Natalia had either.

At 6:00 a.m., a vehicle stopping in front of our duplex prompted me to open the venetian blinds. Natalia's mom exited her car. She strode up the walkway with uncertainty and apprehension on her face. I pulled the front door open at the same instant she pushed the doorbell. She came in.

"Hi," Martina said. "Natalia called me."

I nodded and remained mute.

"She said you were having another one of your episodes."

"Bonkers" would've been my chosen term for my episodes. "Meltdown" seemed appropriate, as well, since plainly I'd gone nuclear.

Shame lowered over my head like a bonnet hood in a beauty salon. When Natalia phoned my ex-wife, my gut soured in self-loathing, but I understood her urgent need to do so.

Natalia stepped into the small dining area of our duplex. The length of her pink-colored pajamas bunched at her bare feet. Tears rushed to her eyes and she began to wail at the sight of her mother.

"He just wants me to be perfect, Mom."

"Wha—" My jaw slackened. My mind couldn't recall anything said about wanting her to be perfect.

"He wanted me to vacuum the floor, and it wasn't good enough for him." Sobs punctuated her words and tears pooled at the bottom of her eyes.

"I never said a thing." My head pivoted from my daughter to her mother.

A memory of Dad's violent yanking of a broom from my hands and dashing it on the floor as he unleashed another tirade resurfaced into my mind.

When Natalia undertook a household chore, I believed I rarely talked about it. In fact, I held back from asking her to perform household duties. I'd felt so put-upon by Dad's constant directives that asking my daughter to do even the smallest thing seemed excessive.

Natalia's claims echoed in my being. Dad demanded that I be perfect. Whatever I did for him was never good enough. My own daughter voiced the same things about me.

Martina moved closer to our daughter and posed with folded arms to appraise me.

Meltdown

"Mom, I just want to be with you. I don't want to stay here anymore." Natalia's eyes brimmed with tears as she gaped at her mom.

A loose floorboard cracked in the foundation of my heart, sending the footing of my life plunging down. "But I . . ." was all I could muster.

"I don't think she can live here with you now," Martina asserted in a universal appeal from a mother demanding to protect her child.

The words seared my core being. A surging tide pushed me toward jagged rocks.

"No. Don't do this to me." I'd never pleaded for anything. Ever. Until now. "Don't take my daughter away from me. Please, you can't do this." My worst fears were being realized.

"Maybe after she has some time away from you, we can talk about her coming back."

My stare shifted from mother to daughter. There was nothing to say to make it better. Though never a hand was raised to Natalia, I had not provided her a secure or nurturing environment. Natalia had a sullen and withdrawn father, a caregiver unable to control his anger. It was the only way of life I knew.

"I don't think this is a healthy environment," Martina continued. "I have to make sure she's safe." She nudged our daughter: "Natalia, go get your things. I'll take you to school."

My breath became shallow and I tried to breathe, trying to hold myself together. The only person I cared about in life was about to leave me. In what seemed an instant, Natalia returned to her mom's side, her backpack hanging from her shoulder.

"I'll call you in a day or two." Martina turned to the door with Natalia in tow.

The door shut behind them with deafening finality. I observed through the dining room window as they got into the car and disappeared down the street.

I staggered to the entrance hallway and sagged like an unwatered houseplant. My world collapsed. I pressed my forehead against the cool paint of the wall and watched a rush of tears drop from my face and disappear into the carpet.

Every day as a youth, I had promised myself that I would never treat my own offspring as I was treated. The realization that I'd become just like Dad was more than I could bear.

Despite my love for my daughter, despite my will for a different outcome, a sobering truth set in. I had failed—completely and miserably. Wrenching sorrow overwhelmed me. I admitted to myself that I had placed the eggshells on the floor she stepped on.

"I can't do this, God," I breathed. "I can't escape my past."

I sank to my knees. My willpower was spent and useless.

"I've tried so hard. Please, help me."

53

A Still, Small Voice

During the next week, I took my lunch breaks at one o'clock to seclude myself. On a bench at a small park adjacent to my office, I sat alone. Sunshine and a soft breeze did nothing to calm my inner storm.

It was my week to have Natalia, but she stayed at her mom's. Although our regular schedule would resume in two weeks, the idea that it might be better for my daughter to permanently live away from me needed serious attention.

My twice-per-week psychotherapy sessions for the last year put perspective on my mental state. One counselor treated me for clinical depression, but my issues seemed so deep-seated that talk therapy seemed ineffective. I had stopped PTSD sessions with another counselor because there were no results. Chronic pain prevented me from engaging in the activities I most enjoyed.

At over fifty years old, mine was a lifetime of struggle. My future didn't look any better.

"This isn't going to end well," I bemoaned to God. Plans for an early, final exit from this life once again formulated in my brain. *What would I do when I saw Him?* I wanted to know why my life had been filled with affliction. *What would He say?*

Despair and anguish saturated my being. Self-destruction would free my pain.

Then a discernible voice, that was somehow not a voice, welled up within me: *You're going to be all right.*

I looked over my shoulder. No one was there.

In the afternoon sun, a small tear escaped the corner of my eye and ran down the side of my face.

"Thank You," I uttered audibly to the Creator who made Himself known to me. I felt more at peace than I had in a long time.

Days later after dinner, I hovered over the dirty dishes in the kitchen sink and reflected on my routine day at work. But in every unfocused moment between reviewing a purchase order, answering the phone or an email, or meetings with coworkers, what God had said to me replayed in my mind: *You're going to be all right.*

Warm water from the faucet flowed onto the plates, drinking glasses, utensils, and cookware the same way His message poured into me. His assurance resonated not as imaginary or a product of wishful thinking, but as something real. God had spoken to me when I plumbed the depths of my sorrow.

It was not the first time I'd communicated with God. On my thirtieth birthday, on bended knees, I had asked to feel His presence. His love engulfed my being, causing me to gasp. As quickly as it came, it receded.

Back then, it seemed to be a one-shot deal. Not until more than twenty years later did I feel His presence again. As a young man, I didn't know what to do with His wordless, all-encompassing love, or how to ask for it again.

This time was different. The Creator had spoken to me in audible words: "You're going to be all right." I was as certain it was Him as anything I'd ever known. But I wondered, *Would God continue to talk to me? Would His presence and reassurance signal a change in my life?*

The setting sun shone brightly into my duplex. An impression nudged me that something was different. I never smiled without good and apparent reason, but I found myself smiling. Why the smile now, especially in the aftermath of my blowout with my daughter who remained at her mother's house?

Something was different. Unmistakably so. I was sure of it. And slowly, the realization of an unfamiliar, encompassing sensation settled on me.

My depression had disappeared!

Melancholy had always swirled in my spirit in a never-ending carousel of hopelessness and misery from which there had been no escape. Depression had continually hovered over my waking life and invaded my dreams.

Now there was no gnawing sadness. *Where were the ever-present signs of gloom and despair?*

A burden eased and an unrepressed lightness in my soul sprang forth. My mind's eye pictured the bottom level of my past. The basement floor contained a trap door that at times disintegrated beneath me, sending me into a free-fall spiral into a cold, unforgiving ordeal of mental and spiritual anguish. God had sealed the trap door, never again to be opened.

After a lifetime of wretchedness and struggle, God had lifted my depression. It vanished and was gone as if it never before existed.

54

Bible Study

"**B**oy, were you lost in the wilderness." Patricia, my coworker from the other end of the building, shook her head. I had told her of my thirty changes of residence in the same number of years. "The Israelites wandered in the desert for forty years, though," she said.

Why would the people of Israel wander in the wilderness for forty years? I barely understood my own relocations.

Beth, my next-door coworker, had summoned Patricia at lunchtime to begin our first Bible study session in my office. In the fifth grade, I attended a Billy Graham crusade at the Oakland Coliseum with my friend and his dad. When the evangelist invited everyone to ask Jesus to be their Savior, I couldn't understand why so many left their seats.

In the past I'd made a concerted effort to go to church, hoping a place of worship would offer something to improve my life. But I was too self-reliant and stopped going. I needed no one, not even God. My independence was based on distrust of everyone. I didn't trust an unseen and unfathomable God.

Yet God had removed my depression. I wanted to know more about the God who had spoken to me. The lifting of my depression was an enormous transformation, leaving me to want to know why—and why me?

Beth prayed for guidance and teaching from the Holy Spirit.

"Who is the Holy Spirit?" I asked after I looked up from my clasped hands.

"You might have heard of Him as the Holy Ghost, part of the Trinity of the Father, Son, and Holy Spirit."

"So why can't you just ask God and have all of it covered?"

"The Holy Spirit is a counselor and a teacher."

"He has a specific job?"

Patricia read a passage from the book of John, and I tried to follow along. I didn't even know who John was. I'd seen John 3:16 signs while watching football games on TV, but had no idea what it meant. The numbers seemed like code.

"How are you doing?" Beth peered at me.

"I have no idea what she just read."

"It can be hard to understand at first," Patricia acknowledged.

"Do you have a church?" Beth asked.

"You mean do I go to a church?" Christian stuff seemed to have a language all its own. "I've checked out a few, but I'm not sure where to go."

"You can go to my church," Patricia said with a rise in her voice. She was also an Elk Grove resident. "It's larger than some, and there are a lot of good people there. Check out their website and go at least five times, and you'll get a feel for whether you like it or not."

Five times? I doubted I'd last more than two.

It was different from the Catholic churches familiar to me. Its main sanctuary had two large video screens that announced the church's events and provided words for sermons and musical interludes performed by the live band and choir.

Seated at the center of the back row, I preferred to keep everything in front of me. I felt safer and I could leave unnoticed.

My usual instincts to escape were held at bay. I promised myself to go at least five times.

The Bible House bookstore occupied a separate building next to a pool supply store in Elk Grove. I'd passed the Bible House many times in the past, but never gave it a second thought.

This time it was the object of my attention. As I pushed open the glass door, bells hanging from its inside handle announced my arrival. I needed to remind myself that anyone looking at me was probably not a threat. I didn't consider myself a Christian, and I sure didn't know how to look or behave like one. Questions or attempts to help me shouldn't be thought of as interrogation or judgment of my ability

I viewed framed pictures, photos, and banners—each inscribed with Bible verses. A greeting-card section lined the back of the store, and cups, figurines, and jewelry competed for attention.

The clerk behind the front counter wore a pleasant smile.

"Where are your Bibles?" I asked, giving up my instinct to find out by myself.

"There's a wall section here with Bibles." She turned to an area next to the front counter and pointed. "Plus, on the standing bookshelves, we have others. You'll see some in our display areas as well. Is there a particular one you're interested in?"

"I don't really know. My friend told me to look at an NIV to see if I like it."

The objective of choosing a Bible became a daunting task. Most of them were thick. Some were hard cover, and some soft. Some were real leather, and some fake leather. Some Bibles came in their own boxes. The NIV Bible I first pulled off the shelf was heavy and made me wonder how long I could hold it aloft while lying in bed.

"We can have that engraved with your name, if you'd like." The clerk's voice interrupted my decision-making.

"Oh, that's all right," I replied. Why would anyone want their name on a Bible? I'd already know it's mine and could just write my name on one of the first few pages.

Many of the Bibles' pages were thin, and some sported gold edges, which seemed to lend an air of elegance and ornate sophistication. Others had red lettering in various sections, making me believe it'd save me the time of highlighting with a yellow marker.

In addition to the NIV, there were other versions: the English Standard Version, the American Standard Version, and The Living Bible. There were some that announced themselves as new: the New King James Version, the New American Bible, the New Living Translation, and the New Life Version. Like many products claiming newness, I wondered if the Bibles should include "New and Improved" in their advertisements.

The experience felt similar to shopping for breakfast cereal. Should I buy the one with "honey bunches of oats," the one that is "magically delicious," or the one that "Mikey likes?" I refrained from asking the kind salesperson, "Which one is the cornflakes of Bibles?" I just wanted a simple Bible, if there were such a thing.

In the end, I resolved that if one Bible couldn't meet my needs, I'd buy several. A two-toned NIV along with an NIV Study Bible checked the boxes. The study Bible abounded with footnote explanations and maps of different locations. It provided a feel for the culture of the area during biblical times. Also, The New Testament in Modern English and The Message purported to be easier to understand. The Amplified Bible, which contained additional wording and synonyms to help the reader comprehend each passage, encouraged me. I bought that too.

At home, I perused my stockpile of Bibles to get a feel for how each one could impart biblical knowledge to me. My coworkers suggested saying a prayer for knowledge before reading Scripture, but I dismissed that as folly. As far as I was concerned, any wisdom obtained would be a result of my ability to focus and comprehend the readings.

As with any book, I started at the beginning—Genesis. While growing up, I'd been aware of the many cultural references to Adam and Eve, the garden of Eden, the forbidden fruit, and the serpent that tempted Eve. My Bibles gave me a firsthand read of those references, and I read intently, trying to absorb their true meaning.

The sheer volume of pages and chapters within the Bible intimidated me. How would I ever get through it? There was no book jacket or back cover to get the gist or summary of what it was about, so I turned to the last book of the Bible. I wanted to know how it ended. Revelation told the story of an epic future showdown between the archangel Michael and a red dragon, represented by Satan. The Revelation tale was as good as those told in comic books where the battle between good and evil is a constant theme. In comic books, as in the Bible, the good guys always won in the end. I hoped to be alive to witness the combat beneath the heavens.

I closed my NIV Study Bible and placed it on the coffee table, unsure whether any more chapters between Genesis and Revelation needed reading. I already knew what happens. Everyone who's a believer lives happily ever after.

55

Uncovered

Weekly service at Harvest Church became a regular routine for me. I'd make my way to the sanctuary's main entrance when the hallway TV monitors counted down to 10 a.m. Once greeted and seated, I read the church bulletin and waited for the choir. The music provided a rousing start as the choir swayed in unison, singing with passion and joy. Many parishioners embraced the music, some standing with one or both arms upraised.

Sermons covered various topics such as forgiveness and anger. At the mention of Jesus Christ and His teachings, some in the audience shed tears. I couldn't understand why and wanted to know more.

As the weeks progressed, others nodded or waved at me. The head usher, Verlie, usually stopped by my seat in the center, back row, to offer a kind word. I began to live my life in a context I hadn't before.

Although still self-willed and independent, could I become a follower of Christ?

My bright red 1996 Nissan 300ZX two-seater with T-Tops, five-speed manual transmission, and Bose audio system made me happy ever after. My ZX turned the heads of both law enforcement officers and young Asian men who'd taken the lead from the *Fast and Furious* movies to transform Japanese imports into sharp-looking racing machines. Like a fighter pilot in my Ray-Ban sunglasses, I eased into the low chassis, settled into the contours of the leather bucket seat, and fastened the shoulder harness. Pride swelled within me at the sound of the engine's roar. My sports car purred like a tiger. A few pumps of the accelerator made the tiger growl, ready to pounce on the road.

My driver's side seat cover was illustrated with a green sharp-fanged serpent. The reptile posed vertical on white nylon, while two red stripes framed the sides. It occurred to me that it covered my entire back. "The snake has my back," registered in my mind.

The passenger seat cover was bright red, with a red dragon snarling at me on a black felt background. It felt as if the red dragon rode shotgun. Like a passenger or a GPS, it had navigation responsibilities too, directing me where to go.

Halfway out of the garage, I braked and thought about my unwanted passengers, each depicted in the beginning and end chapters of the Bible. I'd unknowingly harbored them for years. Without God as my navigator, I concluded the devil had been routing me toward self-destruction, filling me with doubt and loathing. I blinked in an attempt to see my new reality more clearly. A shiver crawled up my spine.

After drawing in a deep breath, I cautiously steered through the nearby streets. *How, and in what ways, had Satan been influencing me?* A cold sweat broke out on my forehead.

I had to do something with my seat covers. I couldn't sell them or give them to a thrift store. I needed to keep them away from other people. I ripped them out of my car, placed them at the bottom of my trash container, and poured soiled kitty litter on them.

The revelation of the enemy in my life dazed me. I was clearly in over my head—no match for a supernatural being. I needed help beyond regular church services and my own random Bible readings and interpretations. *What was I to do?*

56

Honor Bound

E ach Sunday, a listing in the church bulletin raised my curiosity: *Men's Bible Study: Honor Bound.* I liked the sound of it—bound by honor. My recent understanding about dark influences and the symbolism of the serpent and dragon car-seat covers bewildered me. Maybe through the men's group I'd learn how I was bamboozled by the devil.

Honor Bound meetings were held on the first and third Saturday mornings of each month. Two contact phone numbers were listed. One was for someone named Al, and another for AJ.

For weeks, thoughts of picking up the phone brought numerous excuses to not call. There were groceries to buy, the lawn to mow, and laundry to wash.

Actually, I feared they wouldn't accept me. Plus, why join a group of guys? Dad was one, and my experiences with him taught me to distrust most of them, especially those who tried to tell me what to do, or thought they knew everything, or whose answer to every problem was to get tough.

Even more, I was a self-described loner. My personal history overflowed with unfinished projects and unmet commitments. I usually did things on my own. I'd end up quitting the group anyway, so why make the call?

However, in the hollows of my soul, there existed a longing to belong, to be a part of something—not apart from everything.

My attempt to join Honor Bound would probably fail. Certainly, they'd see that I was in the wrong place and reject me.

I pressed the phone number and heard it ring in my ear once, then twice, then five times. I hoped for unending rings or a voicemail prompt. Maybe then I could move on, telling myself I had at least tried.

"Hello, this is AJ."

"Hello, my name is Pete. I'm calling about the men's group."

"Did you get my name from the program?" There seemed to be surprise in his voice.

"Yeah, from the Sunday bulletin. I'm thinking about coming to a meeting."

"That's great! You'll meet a good bunch of guys. Do you know where we're located?"

"Not really. I haven't been going to the church very long. I've never been in a men's group." I tried to be straightforward, but stomach butterflies threw me off kilter.

"That's okay. I think you'll like it. You can come just to see what we're about."

"What do you do there?"

"After introductions, we usually read Scripture and then discuss it."

"Is it like a conference meeting or a classroom? Do people take turns talking?"

"I'm one of the co-leaders. My partner, Al, facilitates the discussions. When people want to say something, they just raise their hand. It's informal."

"Do I have to talk?"

"Oh, no. No, Pete. You can talk as little or as much or as you want."

"That's good, because I don't talk much."

"That's okay. You can just observe if you want."

"How many guys are there?"

"Sometimes there could be as few as ten. Other times there might be over twenty. Right now, we're in one of the small meeting rooms over by the playground."

"I guess I'll come this Saturday."

"That's good to hear. We start at eight o'clock."

"Okay. Thanks, AJ." I hung up and my chest clenched. Now I had stepped into it. At the risk of shaming myself, there was no backing out.

Saturday on the drive to Harvest Church, my perspiring hands gripped the steering wheel, and my breath increased as if hiking mountains at high elevation.

As usual when going to new places, parking in a far corner of the lot well before the start gave me time to observe other arrivals. They were average-looking guys in all shapes, sizes, and colors. One might bump into them at the grocery store. There was no compelling reason for me to drive away. I'd have to go in.

My reflection on the building's glass hallway entrance door showed a sheepish, anxious face peering back. I took a deep breath in an attempt to calm myself. I couldn't remember the room number. Voices came from an open hallway door. I followed the sounds and took one step inside the room. A few men were seated around rectangular tables assembled into a U-shaped configuration.

"Men's group?" I asked. My heartbeat raced as if in the middle of aerobics exercise.

A few of the guys nodded. One of the men at the top of the U called out, "Welcome! My name's Al Rowlett. Have a seat anywhere." I looked at the empty seats, hoping not to sit next to anyone.

"I'm Pete," I answered while heading to a vacant chair between two other empties.

Al was seated next to a massive human being who gazed at me as I sat down.

"Pete, we spoke on the phone. I'm AJ." AJ stood probably six foot, five inches tall and looked to weigh three hundred pounds. Nothing in his calm voice over the phone conformed to the person I saw. He smiled. "Thanks for coming."

As more people filed in around the eight o'clock start time, most of the seats filled.

"Let's have introductions," Al began. "Just say your first name."

When my turn came, I eked out my name, but regretted that my newness brought unwanted attention. Thankfully, Al and AJ started the

Bible study with little fanfare. I spent the next ninety minutes feeling out of place while trying to comprehend the lesson and discussion. Mercifully, the meeting ended and I stood up to leave. AJ turned toward me.

"You're coming back, aren't you?"

"You're always welcome," Al added.

"I guess."

Actually, I guessed not, but wanted to be discreet and not untruthful if I decided to chicken out by the next meeting.

Making my way to the exit, Curt, an Asian guy, reached out his arm to shake my hand.

"I like what you said about faith," I said, looking for something to say.

"Praise God."

Was he asking me to do something? Praise God? I remained silent.

"Yeah, faith is like that chair—you always have faith that when you sit on it, it will hold you up."

"I suppose so," I replied, flummoxed.

"Coming next time?"

"I think so." Though I thought not.

For the following two weeks, I coaxed myself into returning to the next men's Bible study. I had questions that my own reading or listening to Sunday sermons hadn't satisfied. For one, I still had concerns about the devil. Also, I'd heard of Jesus Christ, but didn't really know Him as the men seemed to. And I was still perplexed that faith was analogous to sitting on a chair.

At the next meeting, AJ tilted his head toward me and Al grinned when I walked in. Yet struggles with self-consciousness and vulnerability accompanied me.

The room had no windows and only one door. I claimed a seat near the entrance and kept a mental note of the men I'd have to navigate around if I needed to slip out. A few familiar faces from the previous meeting and some new ones, about fifteen guys, were in attendance.

"I think introductions are in order. There are a couple of new men here," Al began. At the first meeting, introductions were limited to name only. Everyone seemed to gawk at me, making it difficult for me to sit unnoticed. "Let's go around the room. Just say your name. If you want to tell us more about yourself, you can, but you don't have to." Al nodded at me. I read the glint in his eye as his wanting to hear not just our names from the new guys.

Although used to talking about myself at work meetings, this felt different. My need to issue a smooth, noncommittal introduction conflicted with my desire to articulate exactly what was on my mind. I'd always believed myself to be upfront with people. Plus, the desire to know more about Christianity and how it related to my life became a priority. I decided to address my need to know.

"Kevin," the person next to me blurted out. Most of the men uttered only their names. All heads turned to me.

"My name's Pete. I've been coming to Harvest the past few months," I said in a meek voice. The phrase "the meek shall inherit the earth" was a cliché I'd picked up somewhere in life and didn't know it was from the Bible. I didn't feel much like an heir at that moment.

"I have a daughter who's a junior in high school. I guess that's why I'm here." I sat up straighter and composed myself before continuing. "Our relationship has gone all wrong, despite my love for her and my basing decisions on what's best for her."

I made eye contact with each person and clicked into instructor mode, which gave me confidence. "About six months ago, she wanted nothing to do with me anymore because I've had problems with depression and anger. After suffering lifelong depression, I prayed to God for help. He lifted it as if it never had been there."

Many of the guys were still, unblinking, and listening intently as I proclaimed the power of a transformative God. "I'm not a Christian. I don't know what it means to be one. I've only read a few chapters of the Bible. I don't know Jesus. I mean, I know He's in the Bible, but you talk about Him like He's someone you know personally. I don't understand that."

There, I said it. I took a deep breath and awaited reactions.

AJ's face shone with an expression of pride mixed with wonder. Some in the room leaned forward, while others sat back in anticipation. "Guys, let me tell you something. When Pete called me to find out about our meeting, he asked, 'Do I have to talk?'" The big man let out a soft chuckle and continued. "Pete, thank you for your transparency. You can talk all you want. You never know what's going on in someone's life, even in this room. I'm glad you're here."

Al's beaming eyes locked onto mine. His mouth upturned in a smile. "Praise God," he said. "You're in the right place. Continue to come and you'll learn more about the Bible and Jesus. We're all your brothers here. Each of us is at a different place in our faith. Some of us, like me, have a daughter same as you." Al looked around the room. "Any comments?"

"Draw near to God and He will draw near to you," Kees, a tall Dutch man with white hair, said. It was the second time I'd heard that phrase. The first time had been in church. I had difficulty picturing how to draw near to Him and His doing likewise.

Others talked about being in the Word. What word were they talking about? Maybe I'd ask once the meeting commenced. I ended up listening without uttering another word, but I was focused and interested.

After the meeting concluded, many of the men approached me to offer encouragement and to introduce themselves. Curt resumed his talk about faith and a chair. I understood that one trusts a chair to stay upright when sitting down. I partially made the connection: we can trust God to hold us upright as a chair does.

I was like a baby subsisting on milk, a formula I longed to have.

57

Prayer Interlude

"**I forgot my money.** I'll be right back." Natalia opened the passenger side door and hurried up the stairs. On Saturday mornings, during alternate weeks of an equal-custody arrangement with her mom, the nearby Java Time Donut Shop was our customary destination.

Two weeks after my meltdown, Martina permitted Natalia to resume living with me. My ex-wife had looked at me with pity. In a saddened tone, she said "I don't know if returning her to you is the right thing to do. All I know is a child needs her dad. I can't take that away from her."

"I don't know what I'd do if my visits were limited to every other weekend like some fathers have." My heart ached to reunite with my daughter.

"Natalia loves you, and I know you love her."

"Yes, I can't imagine what I'd do without her. I try so hard to do the right thing."

"I know. I see that. It's just that Natalia gets scared sometimes. You can be unpredictable." Martina looked at me for assurance that our daughter would be safe.

"I know. Every day I replay in my mind what happened, but I'm going to be all right." I hoped God was right when He said, "*You're going to be all right.*" My eyes moistened at the recollection of God's intervention. My heart warmed with gratitude.

With reservations, Martina resigned herself to my rejoining my daughter.

As I imagined chomping into an old-fashioned buttermilk donut, my cell phone sprang to life with the pulsating beat of the *Hawaii Five-0* TV show. Music filled my car's interior. My head jolted upward like a jack-in-the-box.

"Hello?"

"Hey, Pete. This is Al. Is this a good time to talk?"

"Yeah, sure." I expected he'd called to check my interest in attending the next men's group meeting and that would be it.

"We're blessed by your coming to Honor Bound. Your honesty and willingness to learn make us think about our own Christianity. We appreciate how much you care about your daughter. Would it be all right if I prayed for you now?"

"Umm, what do you mean? What do I do?"

"You don't have to do anything. I'm just going to pray over you. Are you in a good place?"

"Uh, yeah. I guess." My gaze fell on the apartment stairs, and my nerves prickled at the thought that Natalia would soon come bounding down.

"Dear Father God," Al began. I lowered my head as I'd seen others do in church. *What is a Father God?* I knew what a godfather is from the movies, but not a Father God. "We thank You . . ." My thoughts swirled. *What would Natalia think of me with head down, eyes closed, and phone pressed to the side of my head?* Al continued, ". . . Your loving hand on our brother . . ."

In the past, I considered prayer nothing more than foolishness and empty promise. Loss of control gripped me. I'd always been self-reliant, but I couldn't interrupt Al and say, "On second thought, I'm gonna pass on your prayer."

I didn't know what to do. I'd never had anyone pray over me. Perspiration moistened my ear as I held the phone close. I didn't know a prayer could last so long!

With my head still bowed, I opened my eyes to sneak a peek at the stairs. I wondered if I was disrespecting the Creator by breaking from my prayer position to refocus my attention on Natalia. The thought of her jumping into the car and seeing me silently huddled over my steering wheel as if napping made me cringe. Al finally said, "Amen."

"Amen," I mumbled. I knew enough to repeat the word, though I didn't know what it meant.

"You have a good Saturday, Pete," Al finished.

The passenger car door swung open and startled me.

Natalia settled into the car seat and looked at me.

"What?" I asked with a deadpan expression on my face.

"What?" she asked in reply. She hadn't noticed my surprise.

"Nothing."

"You look like I surprised you."

"No, just talking to someone from the men's group. Ready to go?"

I backed away from the carport and began a slow drive through our enormous residential complex. *What had I gotten myself into by joining a men's group where its leader actually called to pray for me?*

58

Calls to the Altar

"**My daughter's a** pretty good volleyball player. Right now, she's a freshman playing on the junior varsity team," I said. In a Lyon's restaurant booth, I sat across from David, a guy from the men's group. "The other day, while watching one of her matches, I marveled at the ease with which she not only got to each ball, but kept it from hitting the floor. She consistently executed a perfect pass to one of her teammates."

My church brother listened with his teacup pursed at his lips.

"She made some mistakes, like serving into the net, but I was so focused on what she was doing well, I hardly noticed her errors." What a new way of thinking for me!

My friend waited for my next point before taking a drink.

"I saw only the good in her. This made me think, does God look at us the same way? Does He love us so much that He only sees the good?"

David sipped from his cup and glanced down. After a moment, he lifted his gray-haired head and a smile illuminated his weathered face.

"I like how you see it that way," he said. I felt reassured to be on the right track. "God is love. It's not that He dismisses our mistakes. He just prefers we learn from them. He's like a patient, understanding father who wants more than just the best for us. He wants to guide us."

David was one of the first of many men's group brothers who took me under his wing to teach me about Christianity and a relationship with a God whom I believed in, but knew so little about.

"I'll be right back," I said to Natalia while standing from my seat to make my way to the front sanctuary. Pastor Perry, the senior pastor at Harvest Church, summoned those who wished to make a commitment to Jesus Christ to come forward.

Natalia pressed back into her chair to let me by. Her eyes widened in curiosity. It would be the second time I heeded the altar call, but the first when my daughter would see me going forward.

Determined to go up front over and over if need be, I hungered to be close to Christ, to try to improve my lot in life. Later, I understood that a single acceptance of Jesus as my Savior meant I had received the gift of His salvation.

For most of her life, Natalia had seen me live without wanting or needing anyone's help. As I walked to the front, I wondered if she thought her dad had it in him to be a willing follower of Christ.

Feeling self-conscious, as if all eyes were on me, I made my way down the aisle. During previous altar calls, I watched intently from my seat, interested to see who and how many stepped forward.

As many as twenty gathered, and we stood side by side. Pastor Perry stepped from the stage and addressed the congregation with his microphone.

With the ease of someone who'd delivered sermons for decades, his words and manner reflected his Midwestern roots. He implored the audience to lift a hand, a gesture signifying adoration and connection to a loving God, toward the group of seekers standing at the altar. Pastor Perry's sincerity was evident as he asked the Lord to move in the hearts of those who desired to accept Him.

Waiting with my hands clasped in front of me, I was unsure of what to do or think. This second time before the congregation, I wondered the same as I had in the first: *Would I feel the presence of the Lord? Would I burst into tears? Would a halo appear over my head or a heavenly glow surround me?*

Shadows of my own father's abuse invaded my mind. How could I trust this heavenly Father when I couldn't trust my own? Maybe I wasn't good enough to receive God.

"Let's have a brother stand behind a brother and a sister behind a sister," Pastor Perry encouraged. He instructed individual believers from the audience to come forward, place a hand on a seeker's shoulder, and pray over that person.

Long moments passed. *Does anyone care enough about me to stand behind me?* A glance to the side confirmed hands reaching for others, but not for me. What would the pastor do if no one came to me? I knew from my elementary school years what it was like to be the last one picked for a team.

Then someone placed his hand on my shoulder.

The man stationed behind me prayed for me to surrender my will to the Lord, and he spoke of God's love and patience.

After the murmurs of prayer died down, Pastor Perry closed the service. I turned around to a confident smile from Verlie, the head usher, who always stopped at my back-row seat to say hello and offer encouraging words. That he came forward to pray for me meant a lot.

After I returned to my seat, Natalia studied my face, but said nothing.

During the next month, I kept going to the altar. I hadn't fully received Jesus as Lord. A part of me resisted—the same part that couldn't give up self-will and control—the same part that used distrust as a defensive mechanism.

Although I surrendered to God and pleaded for Him to help when I hit rock bottom with Natalia, the barricade that surrounded my heart rebuilt itself apparently out of sheer force of a lifelong habit to protect myself.

"How often should one surrender to the Lord?" I asked Beth.

"Every day," she said. At the time, I couldn't fathom giving myself up to anyone.

Now, on Sundays when summoned, each altar call was to me an act of surrender. I may as well have waved a white flag in front of everyone.

How much longer would I need to draw near to the Lord so He would draw near to me as it says in James 4:8? That Bible verse was one of the first I heard that appealed to me. I wanted the tears of joy I'd seen in others during worship services. I wanted a connection with Jesus. At the least, I hoped for His quiet voice that I heard when He said I was going to be all right.

I usually arrived early at men's group meetings to grab a seat and gain my bearings before the start. Manuel, a regular attendee, never failed to greet me with a warm hug and handshake either before or after the meetings. One morning, he approached as I poured myself coffee.

"Hello, my brother. Always good to see you." His heavy Peruvian accent and deep, loud voice was enough to wake me without the need for morning caffeine.

"Good morning, Manuel." I set my cup down and embraced him.

"You know, brother, I see you always go up for altar calls. How many times are you going to go up there?" He squared up to face me.

"As many times as it takes," I declared. I drew in deep breaths to steel myself and stared at him with laser-like focus. Frustration spilled from my pronouncement. During all those times at the altar, I hadn't felt God draw near to me.

"Praise God," Manuel uttered. He rocked back on his heels. His eyes grew large and his mouth formed a smile. Since he was a high school math teacher, maybe he viewed me as an upstart, remedial student.

"Yeah, I still want that relationship with Him all of you seem to have." I searched the table for the sugar.

"You know, brother, you remind me of a dog I used to have."

It was my turn to step back. I'd never been compared to a dog—a horse's behind maybe, but never a dog.

"The dog was small and a different color from the others. When he was a puppy, the rest of the litter crowded around him in their box. With this dog at the center of the circle, they protected him. The brothers in the men's group do that for you."

I drifted to my seat acknowledging I'd always been different like the small dog—an outsider—but now it was comforting to know a group of brothers cared for me.

Al opened the meeting with Proverbs 27:17 (ESV): "Iron sharpens iron, and one man sharpens another." He described how, as brothers, it would be good for us to study the Bible together not only at the twice-monthly meetings, but also when meeting someone for coffee.

"When I see Pete going up for an altar call and Pastor Perry asking for a brother to stand behind a brother, I don't see any of us stepping up."

Al halted his lesson when AJ interjected his booming voice into the usually deliberate meetings: "It's usually Al or whoever is sitting toward the front." Beads of sweat formed on AJ's forehead. "This brother is yearning to meet Christ! The next time Pete goes up there, I want to see guys running to stand behind him. This is what it means to have a brother in Christ."

AJ slumped back into his chair.

No one said anything, though a few nodded. AJ didn't glance my way; instead, he sat with his head bowed. I'd never before felt so supported. In hindsight, the brothers who stood behind me to pray during each altar call were a blessing, the unmitigated favor of the Lord.

The next day after Sunday morning service, the foyer was bright and bustling. Some parishioners were leaving, while others entered for the next service. While we headed to the exit, I turned to focus on Natalia, making sure I hadn't lost her among the throng.

Derrick, a tall African American, approached me. He was yet another brother from the men's group who always greeted me whenever or wherever he saw me. He lived nearby, and a number of times we had met for coffee.

"Hey, Pete. How ya doin'?" Derrick said.

"Hi, Derrick." I smiled and shook his hand.

I introduced Derrick and Natalia to each other.

"Did you know he brags on you?" Derrick said to Natalia. His eyes lit up and he grinned.

Derrick's disclosure caught me unawares. The relationship between my daughter and me remained guarded and awkward. I was still not used to complimenting her or sharing what went on in men's group. I was glad Derrick indirectly voiced my appreciation of my daughter for me.

Natalia returned a slight smile and stayed quiet. She had no idea that she was one of the main reasons I sought the men's group.

"Your dad is a good man," Derrick continued. "He's added so much to our men's group." He seemed overjoyed to meet my daughter. My heart warmed. I was happy my daughter got to meet the type of person I had befriended in church. I hoped she was seeing that I was trying to become a better father and person.

My church brother meeting Natalia for the first time reminded me that she had grown up to be a gorgeous young lady. One time when she was a high school freshman, I picked her up from school. As she walked across the grass to my car, her long black hair swayed from side to side, her gait was easy, and she appeared to walk in slow motion. *These boys have no chance. They're going to fall all over themselves vying for her attention.* I wondered if I had a stick big enough to beat them away.

In the day-to-day world outside of church, men of all ages stared unashamedly at my daughter, many scanning her from head to toe, gazing at her for far too long. It was to be expected from school-age boys, but with some men who were well into middle and senior years, I felt repulsed and wanted to punch them in the face.

The guys at church, on the other hand, were sincere and genuine, happy to merely meet my daughter. The brothers in Christ represented the definition of men worth emulating. Their examples went a long way toward teaching me how to be a man of God. I continued to attend church services and Honor Bound meetings on a regular basis, craving what they had. I desired to be what they called a servant of the Lord.

They would also educate me more about the entity known as the enemy.

59

Tupperware Lid

While Natalia loaded the dishwasher, I cleared the dinner table. As usual, both of us kept to ourselves. Our mealtimes were normally subdued and short on conversation. If I asked about her day, her answers were usually nondescript and strained. I believed she regarded me as I had regarded my own father.

Leftovers from our evening meal remained on the stove to be put away. Natalia scooped stir-fry vegetables into a plastic container.

After wiping the counters, I walked to her side to help finish. As she placed the final scoop into the Tupperware, I reached for the rectangular lid, but was surprised when the lid snagged. It had caught on the still-hot burner grate and partially melted and warped. The burned area resembled a preschooler's swipe of finger paint on paper. Translucent light shined through the thinned plastic where it had scorched on the burner.

I paused in dismay. Natalia peered at the lid in my hands. She looked as if she were seated in a movie theater watching a horror movie, and I was the villain. The pupils of her eyes widened while her lips pressed into a single horizontal line. She slumped and seemed to have stopped breathing. She was bracing herself.

Memories of past eruptions flitted through my mind. What would I do now? Fling the plastic top across the room like a misshapen Frisbee? Dunk it into the trash bin like a basketball while yelling choice expletives?

Images of what my own angered expression must have looked like filled my mind. I'd have slits for eyes, with my jaw jutting and hardened, and my forehead creased with blood vessels. Or I might say nothing and stare in extreme disappointment at her with my arms folded.

I retreated to the hallway and leaned against the wall to consider my response. Memories of Dad rushing to his room to retrieve one of his belts loomed fresh in my mind. I wished for my daughter to avoid the same terror of impending doom I had experienced.

"No, Satan. I can't let you use me anymore," I whispered to my unseen enemy. "You've held on to me all this time through my anger. This ends now."

I took a moment to compose myself.

As I walked back into the kitchen, Natalia remained paralyzed in the same position as I had left her. With her face turned away from me, I sidled next to her.

"That's okay," I said softly. "Mistakes happen." I scarcely believed those words were coming from my mouth. "It's just a piece of Tupperware." I opened a cabinet and took out a matching lid.

Natalia glanced at me. She said nothing, but placed the new lid on the container. After putting it in the refrigerator, she walked away.

I never told her the reason or source of my change of heart.

Weeks later, Honor Bound listened to my praise report.

"The last time I was here, the subject was about how the devil uses anger as a foothold to keep us close to him." My voice cracked with emotion. "As some of you know, I was raised in a household filled with anger."

The men listened intently.

"I realized the enemy had me right where he wanted me. He isolated me and kept me away from others, including my daughter."

I recoiled, but in the next moment gathered myself. "I told myself, 'I can't do this anymore.' I can't let Satan use me any longer. He's used me most, if not all, of my life."

"Praise God," one of the guys said.

Al beamed at me. Others shared knowing smiles. Over the last year, they'd witnessed my spiritual growth.

"When I told my daughter, 'It's okay. It's just a piece of Tupperware,' she didn't say a word. I'm pretty sure she wondered, 'Who is this guy? What have you done with my dad?'"

The men erupted with laughter.

Phil, someone I had spent a lot of time with, said, "I'm amazed, brother. God is doing a work in you. You've grown right before our eyes." The look on his face reflected pride and bordered on glee. On his way home from his job at UC Davis, his route took him past my corner house. Almost every day, I'd hear two beeps from his sports car when he drove by.

Acknowledgments of support from people like him meant the world to me.

The Holy Spirit continued to educate and feed me in unexpected ways.

60

Unique Eunuch

The modern remake of the *Hawaii Five-0* television series turned out to be as entertaining as the one from the '60s. I'd always enjoyed the upbeat theme music and gorgeous island vistas.

In both versions, when Detective Steve McGarrett instructed, "Book 'em, Danno," at the end of each show after the bad guys were apprehended, all seemed right with the world.

Natalia and I were watching a recording of the previous week's episode.

In one scene, McGarrett strolled down a sandy incline, departing from a witness's house after questioning. A visiting detective, with beauty pageant looks and long blond hair, walked by his side. I suspended belief that female detectives in modern television dramas were portrayed in realistic fashion as eye candy.

"My dad loved my boyfriend," the female detective said to McGarrett.

"What, was he a—" McGarrett turned to her in mid-stride, squinted, and smirked.

"What'd he say?" I asked Natalia.

Natalia shrugged.

I hit the VCR's rewind button. My ears perked during several attempts to capture Detective McGarrett's one word to describe his partner's former boyfriend.

The week before, Natalia had announced that she had a new boyfriend, so I sought to determine what characteristic a father desired in his daughter's suitor.

"I think he said *eunuch*," I concluded.

"What's that?" Natalia asked,

"I don't know." My vocabulary didn't include the word.

I searched and found its likely meaning. In biblical times, *eunuch* referred to a castrated male employed to oversee a royal female's bed quarters. No wonder McGarrett kidded his partner about why her dad loved her boyfriend. I imagined many dads would like their daughter to date a neutered guy.

At dinnertime, I mentioned my findings to Natalia. If I'd learned the meaning of eunuch prior to her recent boyfriend announcement, she could be sure I'd have asked the same question as McGarrett: "What is he, a eunuch?"

Honor Bound reconvened a week later.

Al paused and looked at his open Bible. He waited until we'd settled into our seats for the start of our study.

"Today we're going to talk about Philip. We're not going to be talking about Philip and the Ethiopian eunuch, which is another story, but we're going to talk about Philip."

Did he say eunuch? I rewound Al's sentence in my head. Why would the word *eunuch* again be brought to my attention, days after learning its definition?

After men's group, I hurried home to read Acts 8:26–40 in the Bible.

An angel of the Lord instructed Philip, an apostle, to go along a desert road that went from Jerusalem to Gaza. The Spirit directed him to go over to a man sitting in a chariot. Philip discovered an Ethiopian eunuch reading the Bible. Philip asked him, "Do you understand what you are reading?" (v. 30).

The eunuch was engrossed in reading the book of Isaiah and was unsure whether the Scripture referred to the prophet Isaiah or described someone else. The royal servant answered, "How can I, unless someone guides me?" (v. 31).

Philip next preached Jesus to him. As Philip and the Ethiopian went farther down the road, they came across some water. The eunuch exclaimed, "See, here is water. What hinders me from being baptized?" (v. 36). The eunuch ordered the chariot stopped and Philip promptly baptized him.

I understood that story. The same question the eunuch posed to Philip now came to me: "What prevents me from being baptized?" Over the past year, I'd regularly attended Sunday services and rarely missed a men's Bible study. I'd met with many of the men over coffee to discuss Christianity, attended classes at the church, and regularly read the Bible. It had become clear to me that by way of a TV crime drama, the Holy Spirit was inviting me to consider my own baptism. My heart warmed with assurance.

Since the calendar had just turned to a new year, I expected to find an upcoming water baptism on the church's online schedule. Instead, no baptisms were scheduled for January. None for February. Only in late March.

Maybe I was mistaken. Maybe God hadn't desired me to be baptized.

The following Sunday, while the choir began singing, I sat with the church bulletin in hand and turned to the announcements. One of them read: "A water baptism class is scheduled next Sunday, mandatory for those who want to be baptized on the following Wednesday."

My spirits lifted. I was back in the game. This information hadn't made it to the church's website calendar.

After service, I reported to the Welcome Center to sign up for the water baptism class.

On exiting the building, I imagined Jesus sitting on His throne, then turning to one of His angels, grinning while He joked, "Book 'em, Danno."

61

A New Creature in Christ

A round, cobalt-blue, four-person hot tub like one I once envisioned owning sat in the middle of the Harvest Church stage. Energy costs, maintenance, and how often I'd actually not use it had made me decline. From my seat in the third row, I could hear it hum. Amid swirling water, wisps of steam rose upward.

Under intense lights, Pastor Perry welcomed each baptismal candidate. Each person who stood on stage was nervous with joy—or maybe anxious about speaking into the microphone. When asked why they wanted to be baptized, many looked toward the ceiling as if searching for answers. Applause accompanied each believer at the mic, turning into loud cheers after Pastor Perry lifted each one out of the water.

Thirty-two of us were being baptized. Associate pastor Randy directed us from youngest to oldest. Another associate pastor, Eddie, held a microphone for us to give our testimonies. At fifty-five years of age, I would be one of the last summoned. When the last half dozen remained, Pastor Randy sat next to me.

"You ready?"

"I'll be all right once I get up there."

"Just remember, you'll have about thirty seconds to answer each question, and then Pastor Perry will baptize you.

"Is the water cold?"

"It's like a warm bath," Pastor Randy said with a grin.

My turn came. Apprehension scattered through my being like fallen leaves hoisted by a gust of wind. I walked to the on-deck location, partly hidden from the direct lighting. For the first time that evening, I became aware of the audience and was surprised by the number of spectators who had filled the church and would witness the biggest plunge of my life.

Hoping to remember everything I wanted to say, I had prepared extensively for the two questions each of us was to be asked.

"Our next participant is Pete Cruz," Pastor Eddie announced. "C'mon up, Pete."

My steps to the stage were careful and deliberate. The event took on a surreal quality as the stage lights were overwhelming and my ears seemed to plug.

I was too disoriented to make out a vague murmur from the crowd until I heard, "Pete." I snapped out of my daze to hear the men of Honor Bound chanting, "Pete! Pete! Pete!"

"Sounds like you have a lot of fans out there," Pastor Eddie said into the microphone. I stood at his side and looked at the crowd. Two video screens, as imposing as those at drive-in theaters, projected my oversized, mortified, and embarrassed image.

"When did you proclaim Jesus as your Savior?" Pastor Eddie asked. He tilted his mic toward me. The cameraman stepped toward me for a close-up.

"It was about a year ago at an altar call here."

The pastor kept holding the mic to me, but withdrew it once he saw I had nothing more to say.

"Okay, good," he said.

I had practiced repeatedly, but in this moment of lights and a gazing crowd, my well-rehearsed words got lost. All my experience in public speaking as an instructor meant nothing.

"Why do you want to be baptized?" Pastor Eddie asked. Again, he thrust the mic toward me.

"This is a declaration of transformation of my life that signifies my commitment as a follower of Jesus Christ." I'd remembered that much from my prepared script.

I peered at the crowd to catch my breath, but breath eluded me.

All eyes were on me. They waited. Pastor Eddie waited. I waited, until a voice, yet not a voice, spoke in my head. One time I had asked Phil if the Holy Spirit yells at you. His reply was a simple "Yes."

A New Creature in Christ

"*Tell it like it is!*" the Holy Spirit urged, loud and clear.

I gulped. "I've had a difficult life. I grew up in a severely abusive environment, mentally and physically. As an adult, I was diagnosed with acute clinical depression and PTSD. I couldn't control my anger and depression, and I hit rock bottom when my daughter didn't want anything to do with me anymore. I pleaded to God for help. He lifted my depression as if it were never there. That is why I've become a Christian. I want to be baptized as a follower of Christ."

"Okay, go ahead to the tub," Pastor Eddie said as he nodded toward the water.

"I'm not finished." I stepped closer and reached my hand over the microphone's head, covering it.

"He says he's not finished," Pastor Eddie announced in a befuddled tone. He looked to Pastor Perry.

Pastor Perry gazed at him and then glanced at me. He nodded an affirmative to his associate pastor to allow me to continue.

Pastor Eddie lifted his mic back to me.

"I want to thank Honor Bound, the men's group here at Harvest Church."

Whistling pierced the large room.

A few of the guys yelled, "Peeete!"

"They have shown me how to be a servant of Christ."

A couple of the men stood and clapped.

"Finally, I proclaim through my baptism today that I have a new life as a follower of Christ. My baptism is a symbolic gesture to the Enemy, saying he can't have me."

I was finished.

"Okay," Pastor Eddie said. "Go ahead to the hot tub."

The warm water enveloped me from the waist down. Although dressed in a T-shirt and swim trunks, I felt naked and vulnerable. *Had I said too much? Was I out of line?* On the video screens, I looked like a little boy who'd peed the bed.

I assured myself that I had done as the Holy Spirit directed.

Pastor Perry leaned toward me from his stool beside the hot tub. Kindness and compassion etched his face as he fixed his eyes on me.

"Would you point out your daughter? Where is she sitting?" He sat erect and scanned the crowd.

How would Natalia react to my putting her on the spot? She sat in the middle of the back row, where we always sat. It comforted me to see my Christian coworker, Beth, one seat away from her.

"There. Her name is Natalia."

The camera zoomed to Natalia and projected her onto the two big screens. She half-raised her hand. She appeared to be curious, but not embarrassed.

"The Holy Spirit is saying the word 'more' to me. 'More,'" Pastor Perry said. The lines in his forehead creased. He straightened in his stool. "Extend your hands toward Pete in prayer." A sea of hands reached toward me.

I didn't catch a word of what Pastor Perry prayed, but the outpouring of love overwhelmed me. Some parishioners were deep in prayer, eyes closed, intently interceding to God.

Pastor Perry suggested I hold my nose as he pressed his forearm to my back. He immersed me in the warm water. When he lifted me to the surface, water cascaded down.

Again the men's group chanted, "Pete! Pete! Pete!"

Kevin from the men's group handed me a towel and motioned me to the other side of the stage. I moved slowly to an adjacent darkened staging area.

I shivered and toweled myself. After exposing my innermost secrets about myself and my life with Natalia, lingering nervousness also kept me trembling.

In moments, a line formed in front of me. Al was one of the first of my greeters. He wrapped his arms around me and offered encouragement and congratulations.

Many from the men's group queued. The awe of the occasion overtook my senses. Women and children lined up too. One gentleman from the men's group came with his school-age daughter who had asked him for an introduction. Another woman, a member of the choir, revealed that her brother suffered from depression and asked if we could talk sometime.

At the pulpit, Pastor Perry looked concerned. Likely, he wanted to proceed with the program without the distraction that the lineup seemed to present. He continued despite the well-wishers who waited to speak to me.

In no way had I expected my baptism to turn out the way it did. With the Holy Spirit's urging, I told it like it was. That night, the old passed away and I became a new creature in Christ.

62

Pleased

I had often observed various rallies at the state capitol during my breaks or lunch times because I worked only a few blocks away. So after work one day, I attended a Christian rally at the capitol. I wanted to learn more about current political issues, and was curious which politicians supported a Christian agenda.

The next day I pulled into a parking spot at 7:20 a.m. If I were to arrive at my building after 7:30 a.m., street parking spaces wouldn't be available within one block of my office.

Because of chronic pain in my feet, I was glad to find parking close by, and having a disabled-parking placard enabled me to park in metered spaces without time limitation.

As I stepped out of the car, something seemed different, causing me to stop. Haze lingered in the sky.

Sensing a difference not only outside but within, I remained still. Nothing stirred inside me, but I felt filled in mind and spirit—contented.

Skyward, a rainbow arched over the tall office buildings. Other people gazed upward as well.

After arriving at the second floor, I stopped at Beth's office.

"Hey, Beth. You know what? There's a rainbow outside."

"Oh yeah?" She craned her head to look outside her window. "I can't see it from here, but I can see people looking up. How are you doing?"

"I went to that Christian rally at the Capitol after work yesterday."

"How was it?"

"It was all right. It was interesting to see how Christianity and politics go together."

"That's good you got something out of it. These days there are a lot of forces working against Christianity."

"Yeah, I'm glad I went. When I parked my car this morning, I felt something. I don't know if it was the Holy Spirit or what. It was just a contented feeling, but I can't put my finger on why."

"Let me know if you figure it out."

My enlivened state of mind remained throughout the day. My sense of fulfillment was more than self-satisfaction. The feeling seemed part of my inner self.

Between reviewing work orders, scenes from the evening before at the capitol, and two weeks prior when I had ridden with a group of Christian motorcycle enthusiasts, replayed in my mind.

I'm pleased with you. The thought drifted through my mind as effortlessly as a cloud moving across the sky.

That thought couldn't be mine. Why would I say "I'm pleased with you" to myself?

At the break, I rushed next door.

"Beth, I think I know what happened. That feeling of being filled and contented I was talking about?"

She nodded.

"It's the Lord. He told me He's pleased with me. Maybe it's like a father's pride in his son."

She looked at me without comment.

"He knows I usually hightail it out of here after work, but instead I went to a Christian event yesterday evening. By my joining a group of Christian bikers at the Capitol two weeks ago, He saw my growth as a Christian."

Her eyes brightened.

"I didn't recognize the feeling because it's a feeling of pride. Our Father is proud of me. I didn't know what it was at first because rarely, if ever, did that kind of praise come from my own father. The Lord is showing me the delight a father has in his own child."

I'd finally experienced the unequivocal love of God for myself.

Pleased

"You know, Pete," she peered into my eyes, "I've told people about you. I told my sisters and some Christian friends, 'There's this guy at work. His name is Pete. He came from a terrible background. I regard him as a living miracle.' Christ saved you."

Beth smiled widely and her eyes moistened.

In the past, tears filled her eyes because of her personal, loving relationship with Jesus Christ. But this time, her tears were for me.

Beth had planted the seed. She'd been a witness and instrument of God's transformative power in me.

63

Namesake

ominique, one of the guys at Honor Bound, came to a few meetings wearing a men's basketball T-shirt from Delta, a junior college in the area. He was always the tallest guy in the room.

After one meeting, I approached him and felt as if I were standing next to a redwood tree.

"Do you play at Delta?"

"Oh, no. I'm a coach for the men's team. I played college ball at Sonoma State."

"I love basketball. We should get together for coffee."

Since I was somewhat of a basketball fanatic, it didn't surprise me that we hit it off.

Dominique had played professionally in Belgium and played on free-agent teams vying for opportunities to try out for NBA teams. And at 6'6", he stood out.

Our discussions also covered subjects ranging from Christianity to politics to relationships to business. We frequently sat for hours at coffee shops, sometimes until closing.

Because Dominique was close to twenty years my junior, I believed his knowledge of professional basketball spanned perhaps as far back as the '80s, during the heyday of Michael Jordan, Larry Bird, and Magic Johnson. I didn't expect his NBA familiarity to reach into my era, so I asked him, "I know it's before your time, but have you heard of Pete Maravich?"

"Basketball purists know he was one of the greatest of all time," he answered with the seriousness of a TV news anchor.

"He averaged forty-four points per game in college, and that's before the three-point line," I said. "He was one of the first to dribble and throw passes behind his back. I spent countless hours on the playground honing my game after his."

"He was a triple threat: scoring, passing, and dribbling." Dominique keyed on my enthusiasm. "Some coaches still use his videos for training during practices."

I laughed because many regarded Pete Maravich as just a showman, not skilled fundamentally.

"I didn't really look up to anyone growing up. But him I looked up to. I don't know if I've told you before, but my real name isn't Pete. It's Pacifico. I never took to that name, though. Only my teachers used it. My family nickname was Peewee, and kids in the neighborhood called me that too. I always detested it. It made me feel so small. So when I was sixteen, I named myself Pete, after Pete Maravich."

"Really?" Dominique replied. He raised his eyebrows, and an earnest expression etched his face. "He died doing what he loved—playing a pick-up game of basketball."

"I heard it was at a church playground or something."

"It was a Christian church. He died in the arms of James Dobson—you know, the founder of Focus on the Family?"

"Do you mean to tell me Pete Maravich was a Christian? My boyhood idol, the man I named myself after, was a Christian?" I leaned forward, wide-eyed.

"He did a few Billy Graham revivals. You might be able to find them on YouTube. They're pretty good."

The notion that my namesake was a believer washed over me. I stared at the ceiling.

"I don't know what to think. I never gave it a thought he'd be a Christian."

"In fact, Pete Maravich had said, 'I'd rather be known as a follower of Christ than as a famous basketball player.'"

Namesake

Dominique's statement provided an exclamation point, bringing it home for me.

I recalled the Asian girl I'd met almost forty years earlier among the orchards of San Jose. She said, ". . . I feel that I want to call you Pete," and she disappeared into thin air. I believed she had been sent to deliver a single message about my name.

"It feels like I've come full circle. It affirms me, knowing I got my name from someone I looked up to, someone who was also a Christian."

"God does that," Dominique said. "Even in the Bible, "Peter" was not his given name. He used to be Simon until Jesus named him Peter, the rock of the church."

The God I had come to know left me in awe. He affirmed my existence. I realized He was always with me, even in San Jose.

He intended for me to be named Pete.

64

Two for One

The end of Natalia's high school career loomed on the horizon. She had set her sights on applying to a University of California school, but her combination of GPA and SAT or ACT scores didn't meet admissions requirements. She resolved to bolster her grades at the local junior college and then apply to a UC campus later. With that in mind, she completed registration for her first-semester classes at a community college.

One school, Biola University, continued to send her inquiry emails. An admissions counselor also left messages on her cell phone. Like Natalia, I'd never heard of Biola University.

And although I'd become a full-fledged Christian, I didn't understand the value of attending a Christian university. I later discovered Biola was a nationally renowned institute of higher learning where most faculty, staff, and students were professing Christians.

Natalia guessed she must've put her contact information down at a school college fair, which is why Biola approached her. Biola had shortened its name from *The Bible Institute of Los Angeles* when it moved to Orange County and broadened its degree offerings.

"I told my counselor at school that Biola called. I asked her if I should call back. She said I should. So I called them, and they want me to apply."

"That's good. We'll see what happens." Even then, starting at the local junior college met with my expectations.

Weeks later, after school, Natalia stepped in with a broad smile.

"Guess what, Dad? An admissions counselor from Biola called. She said my application was late."

Her enthused demeanor suggested I withhold a lecture about waiting until the last minute.

"She asked me about the admissions letter I wrote and mentioned she had a meeting this morning with the other admissions counselors. She told me they began their meeting praying for me. They want me to go there."

"God doesn't care about deadlines." A familiar welling up of the Holy Spirit rose inside me as my voice cracked. *What school prays for you? What's in the admissions letter that made them reconsider the late deadline?*

Days later, Natalia shared her admissions essay with me. Here, in part, is the last section:

> My father ended up being the biggest miracle in my life. I used to dread the days I would have to spend with him due to his angry and depressed state. Yet if you were to see him now, he no longer possesses the eyes of hate or wears the mask of anger. Instead, all that is left is the love he holds for God and for me. . . .
>
> Seeing his transformation gives me hope for my own miracles. Though there has not been any grandiose event that has magically cured all my problems, God still transformed my life. The Lord blessed us, and His grace is amazing. With His subtle and gentle influences within Dad and me, I know the changes are permanent. Through it all, my own father, whom I used to hate, brought me to the Father. Now I want to be with the Lord all the time. . . . I believe the Lord has guided me to a path of righteousness, a path that begins with this first step in applying for admission to Biola University.

Tears flowed down my cheeks. The effect my pursuit of God had on my daughter had escaped my notice until I read her essay. She'd gone to church with me throughout her secondary school years. She'd met many of the guys from men's group. In fact, Al Rowlett, Honor Bound leader, had provided her a written reference as part of her application package.

I once cried in anguish when my daughter wanted to disown me, but I now shed tears of gratitude to a God who granted redemption for us both. I discovered a God who had something bigger and better than what I could conceive. In saving my eternal soul, He went two for one and got my daughter as part of the deal.

Natalia later discovered that her ACT scores were indeed high enough to attend a UC school, but by then it was too late to apply. She speculated the Lord must have helped her read it wrong.

I prayed to know if the Lord had plans to prosper her and not harm her, and to give her a hope and a future as set forth in Jeremiah 29:11. He assured me that indeed it held true for her. Even more so, He told me not to worry. He would take care of her.

The generational curse was broken.

65

Sufficient Grace

"It seems to me that the Bible is a story of forgiveness. That's its main theme." After reading my one-year Bible in fifteen months, I made the remark to Phil, my church brother.

Phil didn't say anything, but nodded in acknowledgment.

I pondered over Mark 11:26: "But if you do not forgive, neither will your Father in heaven forgive your trespasses."

As a new believer, I concluded that if I were to be a follower of Christ, and more importantly, be obedient to Him, I needed to do something I thought I'd never do: forgive my parents. Since Dad passed away long ago, I'd start with Mom. To be meaningful, I felt I needed to travel to Virginia to speak to her face-to-face, and not over the phone or through a letter. She had moved to Cookie's house shortly after Dad died.

On my knees I prayed, "God? Do you think it's a good idea if I forgive my mom?" I later imagined Jesus seated at the right hand of God, saying "Duh!" with an affectionate grin.

It was a difficult question for me given my few interactions with Mom while growing up. In my eyes, her biggest transgression was that she never protected me from Dad.

Yet she would certainly have also been under attack. I supposed Mom felt as helpless as me. Perhaps she shut down emotionally and psychologically and numbed herself in order to survive.

Still, the little boy that was me couldn't understand.

"If you think my forgiving my mom is a good idea, I need to know for sure." I stayed on my knees, talking to God. "Please give me a sign or answer that's unmistakably You. I really don't have the money to fly out there, so I don't think this trip is likely to happen."

In a few days, my West Coast sister, Penny, emailed me: "Hi, Pee-wee. Looking if you might want to visit Mom the week of Sept. 26–Oct. 5. Usually we go to Myrtle Beach on the East Coast for a golf trip, but this year, Cookie and Bill are coming out here to Palm Desert. . . . I'll take care of the airfare to Virginia if you're willing to take care of Mom."

I had my answer.

In September, I arrived early to spend time with Cookie before being alone to care for Mom.

"Mom is really funny," Cookie disclosed. "She has a good sense of humor. People always comment about how kind she is. They say it's in her eyes."

This surprised me because there was nothing funny about growing up with her. Kind? Maybe insofar as she didn't beat the crap out of me or verbally berate me as Dad had.

The next day, we visited my niece Jennifer and her family.

"Who's this? Looks like Grandma, doesn't he?" Phillip, Jennifer's husband, said to his six-year-old daughter McKenna. I'd heard from others that I resembled Mom.

On sitting for dinner, Phillip searched his cell phone for knock-knock jokes and read us one about a dyslexic person.

"What's dyslexic?" the precocious McKenna asked.

"It's where you say words backward," explained her dad.

"Ho," I responded. To my surprise, Mom laughed out loud. She quickly grasped the punchline when I had transposed the letters in "Oh." It took time for the others to get it.

The following week, I was alone with Mom. I prepared her meals and made sure she took her pills. As always, she spent most of her time watching TV. When it was time to eat, I held her hand and guided her to the table. Touching her gave me the creeps. Most days, the only words between us came from the TV.

Each night, I prayed for the Holy Spirit to give me an opportunity to offer forgiveness. It never came.

On the last day of my stay, I was mindful of a 6:00 a.m. flight the next morning. I determined that I wasn't going to have traveled three thousand miles for naught.

"Natalia's in college now. She's going to school in the Los Angeles area." After clearing the dinner dishes, I showed her a picture of my daughter at Biola University.

"I used to live in Los Angeles," Mom uttered. Her eyes brightened at the sight of her granddaughter.

After more stilted conversation, I trudged ahead.

"There's something I want you to know. Growing up for me was very difficult. I think for you it was difficult, too, with Dad."

I could not make eye contact. Instead, I directed my speech off to the side of the table.

"I don't blame you for what happened to me. I forgive you."

I sat in silence, peering to the side.

With not a sound from my mother, I reiterated my pronouncement, verbatim.

More stillness.

Warily, I turned to look at Mom.

"Yeah," she said.

After more gazing at the TV, Mom slowly rose from the table and walked away gingerly, wordlessly; her back receded into her bedroom doorway as she retired for the evening.

What's that about, God?

"My grace is sufficient," He said, before I finished my thought.

There'd be no changing our past. I understood. God wasn't going to reformulate my memories into ones of a happy childhood. I saw that, like her, I had closed myself off for the sake of self-preservation when raising Natalia. And like her, I hadn't expressed feelings to my daughter because I didn't know how.

God's grace came in discovering that humor and kindness were passed to me from Mom. I came to know her as I know myself. His grace allowed me to accept my mother for who she was and move on.

Epilogue

Mom passed away five years after she walked away from me and into her bedroom—the scene forever imprinted onto my memory.

When Cookie's husband phoned me about her death, it didn't register much.

Al, Honor Bound's leader, got wind of Mom's passing, and I fielded unwanted condolence calls from the guys. Although I appreciated their sympathy, their perspectives came from a place of how they would have felt at the passing of their own mothers. I couldn't relate; I hardly knew my mom.

During her viewing, I sat in front of her open casket. My eyes brimmed with tears and my chest heaved as I tried to hold myself together. The finality of seeing Mom lying down lifeless got to me. The little boy in me had held out the tiniest bit of hope that he could bond with his mother. That chance died with her.

At her interment, I mentioned how as a child I'd sit with her on Sunday nights watching the old '60s television show, *Bewitched*. I stationed myself about two feet away from her on the sofa. She never said anything to me and rarely acknowledged my presence. That was our relationship in a nutshell. It was as close as I could get to Mom.

I grieved for the loss of a relationship that never was.

Dad died at the age of 86, causing me to quip, "He 86'd at 86." If he were alive at the time of this writing, he'd be 110. At best, I'd still keep him at a distance. The wounds will always be too deep, the trust unrecoverable. What would I say to him now? I put those thoughts to rest in another unsent letter:

Dear Dad,

The salutation to start this letter is mere formality. The word *dear* is an affectation. It is not related to *affection*, which I cannot find within myself to have for you.

Furthermore, *Dad* is capitalized as a matter of correct punctuation. In the first drafts of my memoir, I referred to you as "my dad," not wanting to credit you in capital terms. I used "Dad" to not throw off the readers, who might have wondered why I didn't refer to you as "Dad." In my mind, you had been lowercase, similar to me always being Peewee.

The effects of your fatherhood influenced my thoughts, feelings, and behavior in profound and powerful ways. I lived in a world based on fear. I pushed back at the world using anger because anger provides an illusion of power and control and creates distance.

Each time you bullied me, you didn't see that I suffered in dejected silence. As a youth, I continuously promised myself that I would never do to my own offspring what you did to me.

Yet it happened.

Though I never laid a hand on my daughter, Natalia, your granddaughter, I had my share of explosive rages. A handful of times was enough to instill fear in her, while for you fits of wrath were a daily occurrence. I regret I couldn't place a consoling or protective arm around her while she grew up. Instead, I gave her the opposite. She learned to fear me as much as I feared you. It's likely she hated me, as I did you.

In my household with Natalia, there were the same expectations to do anything and everything perfectly. I've wondered if your prodding was some twisted way on your part to get me to be a better person. I rarely complimented, supported, or encouraged Natalia. I didn't hug her. In fact, I hardly touched her.

There were a few episodes of out-of-control temper, but I spoke on an even keel when addressing her. Because of that, I mistakenly believed I was a good father.

It was difficult to see beyond myself during those cheerless times. My efforts were insufficient to attend to my daughter's needs. It's likely she blamed herself for my anger and depression.

Through it all, my love for my daughter never wavered. Although I could see our relationship wasn't healthy, I kept her best interests in mind.

Epilogue

With you, I struggled to find genuine concern. Once when I was in second grade, you saw that I had artistic talent because I could draw anything. "Maybe we should send you to art school," you said. Your face conveyed sincerity, a departure from your usual contempt. Another time, when I was in fourth grade, you saw me helplessly flail, trying to fend off physical attacks by Buster and Scoop. "Maybe we should send you to learn karate," you suggested. Your face seemed to show concern. But you didn't follow through either time.

I held on to those incidences, morsels of evidence that you cared about me. Despite all the chaos and carnage, did you love me the same as I love my daughter? I will never know.

I battled demons of your creation. I had terrible nightmares. While I slept beneath my blankets, my body twitched.

Nowadays, the dreamscape is different. I don't flee anymore. I stand and fight. Faceless entities come for me. Underneath my bed sheets, I kick and punch. Sometimes the covers fly off my bed. A few times I've fallen onto the floor. My desire to attack and vanquish these evils is great. In my mind, I know I will win. I've come so far. I don't run away now. I don't dream of the bull anymore, maybe because you're gone.

The Lord also helps me to keep my anger in check. I've always been afraid of it. I feared it would be the same as yours. I didn't get better until I realized that I am not you.

I've learned my lashing out amounts to a desire to protect the part of me that needs to know it is valued and important. I think it occurred the same for you. When I did not perform to your standards of perfection, it impacted you on a personal level. You believed you were being disrespected, devalued, or dismissed when I couldn't attain your expectations of how to behave, act, or be.

Although I'll always be a work in progress, I've been able to move on. Post-traumatic stress disorder and the various fears I deal with are difficult to work through. Before, I thought myself incapable of close relationships or intimacy. When I became a Christian, the Lord whispered to me that I shouldn't be alone. I am now developing stable and enduring relationships. Natalia and I have a wonderful father-daughter relationship. We text regularly and talk on the phone for at least an hour each week. Father's Day, holidays, and other occasions have become special.

I'm 100 percent sure your upbringing was worse than mine. Although you never talked about it, it had to be. I think your issues were so bad that you couldn't help yourself, like I couldn't help myself with Natalia. Your anger consumed you. You were more broken than I.

I've tried to forgive you. Each time you whipped me with a belt, each time you kicked me, each time you screamed harsh and cruel words at me was your choice. I believe you made those choices on a daily basis to hurt me. You never showed remorse. If you'd have said "I'm sorry" just one time, I'm pretty sure I would've forgiven you on the spot. To your dying day, I hoped for an apology that never came.

I'm sorry I'm not yet in a place where I can find forgiveness for you. I don't think I'm angry with you anymore. Maybe I resent you. I wonder how my life would've turned out had I not spent all the countless hours in therapy. I've devoted so much time and energy trying to get better, striving to make sense of my life. I've struggled mightily to overcome you.

I believed that I always had a good heart. The belief that I would get better sustained me. God kept my heart in its right place.

My life is what it is. I wouldn't be the person I am if I hadn't undergone what I did. I'm okay now. My remaining years on earth will be the happiest of my life.

Your son,
Pete

I believe Dad lived with regret and that he never intended for his life to turn out the way it did.

Although I feel sorry for him and believe I understand him, there are still no tears for Dad. I'm still struggling, but I have faith my heavenly Father will enable me to forgive and love my earthly father someday. I will reach the end of my path to forgiveness and reconcile my heart and mind. The thought that I could forgive Dad is light-years away from what I could conceive before. I never believed I could forgive him in my lifetime.

It's apparent to me also that the Lord put many people in my path who cared about me, helped me, and appreciated me, but I couldn't see it at the time. I have been in God's hands, and I'm in His hands now.

The trail's end is on the horizon.

"Now as Jesus passed by, He saw a man who was blind from birth. And His disciples asked Him, saying, 'Rabbi, who sinned, this man or his parents, that he was born blind?'

"Jesus answered, 'Neither this man nor his parents sinned, but that the works of God should be revealed in him'" (John 9:1–3).

Acknowledgments

I imagined I would spend long, solitary hours hunched over my keyboard to write this book. For much of the time, that's what happened. What I didn't foresee was needing anyone's help. I needed lots.

I'm grateful to two psychotherapists, Michael Beckner and Heather McNally, who, as they read my book, will likely recall the many incidences of my past I had disclosed to them during our weekly sessions. They were with me for the entirety of my writing journey. They encouraged me through my doubts and breakthroughs. They provided insight and support. Many times, I just needed to know if my thinking was normal.

I didn't become serious about my writing until I joined a critique group. Twice monthly, we evaluated each other's chapters. During my first meeting, one of the members, Lori, announced from across the table, "You're a really good writer!" I turned to the person next to me and smiled. Lori looked me in the eye. "I mean you," she said. *Me?* Our group usually numbered four or five, as participants came and went. The mainstays were led by Michelle Murray and included Lori Sinclair, Mary Allen, and Jane Daly. Their feedback and support were invaluable. Our meetings were a place of love, laughter, and joy.

Later, I joined a writers' Meet Up group called *Shut Up and Write*. We met weekly at a downtown Sacramento coffee shop for one hour of focused, uninterrupted writing. We introduced ourselves, told what we were working on, and then got to it. I'm amazed by the amount of writing I accomplished in sixty minutes. Each meeting seemed like a personal writers' support group. I'm grateful to all the fellow word artists, whose participants varied from three to a dozen. Many thanks to the hosts, Todd Boyd and Karen Durham, for being there for us.

After I had completed my initial drafts, I turned to people who provided their impressions of my manuscript. I was too close to my story and needed others' objective views. I wanted to know what worked and what didn't. What needed clarification? Did the story flow? Most weren't writers themselves, but were interested readers. My readers were led by Anna Y. Jiang, who read through and commented on each of my three major revisions. Dominique Bukasa, Rick Leach, and Susan Todd evaluated the final version. I'm indebted to them for their clear and thoughtful impressions.

The Mount Hermon Christian Writers Conference, held at nearby Santa Cruz, California, is an annual gathering of nationally known industry luminaries. For years, I put off attending because I wondered if I was good enough. After the first day, I planned to leave and spend the rest of my conference time at the beach. I didn't think I fit in—until I met Edwina Perkins, an editor from the East Coast. She read my first chapter and praised my writing. I'll never forget how she told me how she couldn't help but turn each page. The next rainy day when I walked by, she called me over to speak with her under her umbrella. She implored me to finish my book. She believed in me and eventually introduced me to my mentor, Cec Murphey, a nationally renowned Christian author and speaker.

Cec took my writing to a higher level and pushed me because he believed in my talent. His comments and reviews of my writing were always prompt and on point. But he occasionally emailed, "I pray for you every day. How is Pete doing?" His concern for my well-being was just as valuable as his feedback about my progress as a writer.

Cec's desire to help other aspiring writers prompted the formation of a group of his protégés. We Zoom each month from locations throughout the US and share our writing dreams, experiences, and needs. This group, like its mentor, gives more than it receives. The members are quick to offer support, encouragement, advice, time, and prayer. Thank you, Dr. Katherine Hutchinson-Hayes, for coordinating our monthly meetings, agen-

Acknowledgments

das, and for recording our goals, accomplishments, and prayer requests. Thank you, fellow protégés: Gwen Burton, Sarah Wind, Rodney Combs, John Chisum, and Kelly Fordyce Martindale.

Upon completion of my first draft, editor Peter Lundell, from EA Books Publishing, helped make my story concise and organized. Cec's daughter, Wanda Rosenberry, proofread and edited my final draft.

Many thanks to the wonderful staff at Redemption Press for getting this book into print: Athena Dean Holtz, owner; Jen Fedler, project manager; Dori Harrell, managing editor; Micah Juntunen, acquisitions & marketing director; Lynette Bonner, cover designer; Tisha Martin, copywriter; and all the other folks whose names I didn't get who worked behind the scenes.

I'm grateful to Maribeth Sprague for planting the seed. She'd tell you, "It only took ten years." But in part because of her, I shall forever be a child of God.

From start to finish, God has been there for me. I firmly believe the Lord has arranged for me to meet every person, arrive at every place, and experience and learn from every event in order to complete my writing journey. During some of the times of solitary writing, while hunched over my keyboard, tears streamed down my face as I struggled with the especially difficult instances of my life. The Lord stood next to me, saying, "I'm right here with you." When I doubted, He encouraged me to get my story done. "Finish the book and everything will be all right," He continually nudged.

In the creation of this book, to God goes all the credit, all the glory. This is His story.

An Unsent Letter to Dad

Dear Dad,

June 18, 1991

I am writing to you because I have a lot of things that I need to say about growing up with you and how it affects me now as an adult. I'm writing because I think I know now that I could never talk to you in-person, comfortably. Although a lot of what I'm about to say you may not understand, I just need to get it out, to say it for myself.

As a child my life was hard with you. I never felt comfortable in that household; essentially, I never felt ok. You were always so domineering (I know you don't like that word, but it's the one that fits) and oppressive. It seemed like if you weren't yelling at me, you were hitting me. The rest of the time was spent wondering when it was going to happen again. For example, when working out in the yard, there was an arrangement that whenever you wanted something I would go and get it. Well, one time you asked "where's the short-handled hoe?" And, as always, I literally ran for it. When I came back with it, you shrieked, "I didn't tell you to go and get it! I just want to know where it is!" As a young kid, I knew it was coming. I didn't know it would be just then. After all those times of retrieving things without fail, I knew that eventually even that would not be good enough. And I think about all those times when I would look for things that you requested, I was so fearful and worried about what would happen (to me) if I didn't find them. On that particular time, you threw the hoe at my feet. I don't know if you intended to hit me with it, but for whatever reason, you were successful in terrifying me.

The example I first wrote about was just one of many, many like incidences. Anything done for you had to be absolutely perfect. The copper bottoms of the pots, the painting of the house, the change from Safeway, the irrigation paths for the tomatoes, all were done perfectly. The clear message of my youth was that for anyone to get any attention around here, you had to do things perfectly without question. Well, I held up my end of the bargain, you didn't.

It was very difficult, almost impossible growing up in a situation like that. I was measured not for who I was as a person, but on what I could do as a worker. Further, I could voice no opposition, opinion, or question. As a small child and a young boy, I think I just wanted to know that I was OK; I needed to know that from you. Instead, when I did things perfectly, the message from you seemed to be — "not good enough." Every kid needs to know from his parent(s) that he is OK.

– 2 –

There have been many things about my life at home I've dwelled upon and even cried about. My dog whom always greeted me when I came back from school, one day was gone without a word along with the rest of his things. I wish somehow you could've just pretended he ran away or got run over and then put his things away. You never would even say "Hi" to me or ask me how my day was, or what I was interested in.

I spent a lot time, years, trying to figure you out in the hopes that I would discover that I am OK or even to feel closer to you. But I don't know that I've accomplished any of that. I can't figure out why my birthday was never celebrated. I've seen pictures of others having birthday parties when they were small and even when they turned sixteen. But I just don't understand how your own agenda could be more important than a boy's, your own son's birthday. Just one. When I see little kids, little babies, and think about the one we almost had, I don't think anything could be more important than a new life, a young life, one that was celebrated and appreciated. Not a word was ever said about my birthday. One time I remember thinking to myself, "For my birthday, I get to work in the backyard."

- 3 -

As a kid I always wondered who you are; and, as an adult I felt that I had a right to know. I used to look at your army helmet and ammo box out in the garage wondering what kind of soldier you were or if you had any notable experiences. I've wondered about your life in the Phillipines as a child and how it was for you when you came to the U.S. What was your own family like? How many brothers and sisters? What kind of schooling did you have? where?

Unfortunately, for whatever reasons, you chose to not show yourself. Instead there was bits and pieces and a lot of guessing to fill in the gaps. When we moved to Milpitas (I was 7), you stopped visiting friends or having people over. Whenever we'd do something for Thanksgiving or Christmas, you'd stay in your room. You pointedly told everyone that you would not accept gifts to you for Christmas, Father's Day, or your birthday. Likewise, you never wanted to have your picture taken. I can only guess at the whys and wherefores, but growing up it seemed the message was that you did not want to be a part or to share in whatever good feelings there may have been in the get togethers. It seemed that the only way you wanted to be in my life was to tell me what to do and how to do it.

As I mentioned, I've spent a lot of time trying to understand what happened so that I

-4-

280

might be OK with you and also with myself. I know a lot about the Phillipines and life for Filipinos in the U.S. But it still does not replace the cultural identity I do not have. And looking at it generally, I can only conjecture that your experiences were the same as those I studied. I've also thought that during many years of my boyhood, you were an alcoholic, and you hid it very well. By the way your eyes were bloodshot and ~~glass~~ glazed when you were in a tirade, it reminds me of someone in an alcoholic rage. Ironically, I've seen those same eyes myself when I've been drunk. Many times you would storm out of your room looking to blame someone for something, anything. I have a feeling some alcoholics do that. Were you venting frustration and anger over a hard life? I once thought that you were driving me/us so hard because you wanted us to have a better life than you had. But now I think your obsession to perfection was more out of your need ~~and not so~~ to control and not so much to help us compete in the real world. You always called me the "Last Link" as if whoever came before me had already failed and that I was the only one who could fulfill whatever dreams you had.

But I can no longer, and I am no longer responsible for fulfilling whatever ideas you had in raising me. I can no longer do things out guilt, fear, or shame. at the thought of what you think of them. I no longer can do things thinking that it will meet your approval or get your respect and attention.

Whenever you'd beat on me or yell at me I was always so afraid and scared. But to add on to that, it always seemed as if it was a no-win situation. There was nowhere to run; there were no excuses to be made. If I was able to get away for a brief respite at school or at a friend's you always seemed to be ready and waiting for another chance. To hear again about whatever incredible wrong had been committed the next day, the next week, even the next month is enough to make the most secure person feel small and demeaned. It was humiliating and shaming to have to go through that all the time. It's really tragic for me to ~~had~~ learned those types of lessons.

I can no longer responsible for your hitting me, your problems, your put-downs, your dreams, or your neglect. I can only be responsible for putting my life together in a positive way.

At this point in my ~~life~~, I ~~have~~ had to put my life back together. I have felt very damaged in a large part, if not wholly, due to my upbringing. In the last ten years or more, I've gone ~~through~~ jobs, relationships, and residences ~~looking~~ for something that wasn't there. I'd visit you and other family looking for something that wasn't there. I guess I was looking for feelings, affection, attention, and the security of feeling/knowing that I belonged or was a part of something.

Now, as an adult, well into my 30's I have

-6-

to deal with bouts of depression, a loss of confidence and self-esteem, and not being satisfied that whatever I do is good enough. For example, just yesterday I felt really, really bad that the sprinkler-head I fixed and the side gate were not good enough. Along with that, thoughts of my job, our household budget, and my health seemed to amount to just a terrible failure. Well, today I can see that all those things are good enough right now; yesterdays messages were yours.

Right now I'm trying to make a foundation for a stable, happy, loving and caring home environment with Martina, my dog and cat, and our future children. But, unfortunately, I don't know if I know how; you and my family life never provided me the tools in which to do that.

Right now I have a problem in just talking to people because I don't have confidence in standing alone without a foundation. I can't seem to ask for what I want since I don't trust anyone and I'm uncertain of what it is I want since it may not be good enough. The simplest things such as talking to people about our backyard landscaping, I don't seem to have it within me to assert myself. Sadly, part of me is still afraid of people enough that I don't know how to make or have friends. In the past, I derived a lot of energy and what I wanted from anger and subtle intimidation. But that's not the way for me anymore.

- 7 -

283

I've dealt with a lot of the anger and frustration, pain and confusion that I've felt from having you as my father. I didn't ask for you as my father — you just were. But it'll be a life long process me feeling bad about something like a sprinkler head and then deciding that it wasn't so bad after all. It'll be me apologizing to my own kids after I've berated them for not doing something at the instant or not to my specifications.

I'm not looking for an apology from you or even acknowledgment that anything was amiss from my childhood upbringing. I'm just looking for me to move on. You might even feel guilty or sorry that things happened the way they did. But I can't be responsible for your thoughts or feelings; I can only be responsible for dealing with my past the only way I know how and reclaiming my adult life.

I sorry you and I didn't have the kind of relationship we could have. I don't think it's possible to have anything but a superficial, distant, and occassional one now. The child that I was is still very much afraid of you — the memories of that house are still too strong, and the scars too deep, the wounds too many.

I'll still come by but only once in a while because I don't know that there is anything there for me. And it'll only be on my terms; as I've said I'm moving on with my own life. I no longer tolerate any abuse from you or

–8–

anyone. Whenever it occurs I now have a choice to remove myself from it. I'll continue to send something on Father's Day as I've done in the past, unless there is a strong objection from you. As my father, you just were. I don't know you very well. But if you were to treat my kids nicely, as you've done with others, that would be your choice. In fact, it would be something I would appreciate. I am grateful for what you've provided me. I had a place to eat and sleep, clothing, and I finished school. And, I did learn some values such as self-respect which may be attributable to your upbringing of me.

It is sad, however, that you do not know me. I've done some good things in my life. I really am something.

       —Pewee

ORDER INFORMATION

To order additional copies of this book, please visit
www.redemption-press.com.
Also available at Christian bookstores and Barnes and Noble.

CPSIA information can be obtained
at www.ICGtesting.com
Printed in the USA
BVHW050813300922
648129BV00003B/12

9 781646 458233